Learning 40 Hadiths
and
56 Inspired Stories for Kids

Islamic Book for Kids

Grades 1-7

Prepared and Published by: Islamic Book Store
302 Saad Residancy
M G Road Bardoli
Surat Gujarat
India
394601

Contents

THE PURPOSE OF TEACHING HADITH AND AKHLAAQ

Rasulullah ﷺ has explained the virtues of memorising the Mubaarak Ahaadeeth. In one Hadith he has mentioned:

$$نَضَّرَ اللهُ امْرَأً سَمِعَ مِنَّا شَيْئًا فَبَلَّغَهُ كَمَا سَمِعَهُ$$

May Allah سُبْحَانَهُ وَتَعَالَى brighten up the face of that person who heard something from us (my words – Hadith) and passed it on in the same form that he heard it.

In another Hadith, the following has been reported:

$$مَنْ حَفِظَ عَلٰى اُمَّتِيْ اَرْبَعِيْنَ حَدِيْثًا مِّنْ سُنَّتِيْ اَدْخَلْتُهُ يَوْمَ الْقِيَامَةِ فِيْ شَفَاعَتِيْ$$

That person who learns forty Ahaadeeth from my sayings, I will intercede for him on the Day of Qiyaamah.

Through the blessings of these Ahaadeeth, the mu'allim/ah and the pupils will attain success in this world as well as the *Aakhirah, Insha Allah.*

GUIDELINES FOR THE TEACHER

Keep in mind the following guidelines when teaching Hadith:

1. Object

The object of teaching Hadith is to:

- To make amal and earn sawaab.
- Inculcate the teachings of Rasulullah ﷺ in the lives of our children.
- Memorise the wordings of the Hadith. If the child has memorised the Ahaadeeth and understood its meaning, he/she will Insha Allah remember them on the appropriate occasions and practice upon them.

2. Time

The official Hadith period will be once a week, on a Wednesday or Friday. However, a quick revision of the Hadith should take place daily between subjects. A chart of the new Hadith should be pinned on the board. If the maktab is in a school classroom, the mu'allim/ah may stick the chart on the wall before the class time commences and remove it after madrassah is over. A quick revision can take place between subjects for 1-2 minutes daily. For instance, the Qur-aan Sabak is over and it's now time for Fiqh. Before the children can open their Fiqh books, revise the new Hadith quickly for 1-2 minutes and get the entire class to repeat it together a few times.

3.   New Hadith

When teaching a Hadith for the first time, the following procedure must be followed:

Make the pupils recite the following before each Hadith:

$$\text{قَالَ رَسُوْلُ اللهِ صَلَّى اللهُ عَلَيْهِ وَسَلَّمَ}$$

Rasulullah ﷺ said

- Read the Arabic text word for word at a slow pace so that the correct pronunciation of every letter is clearly heard by the children.
- Read the translation.
- Make at least 3 children, in turns, read the Hadith from the kitaab or the chart. Correct any mistakes. Emphasise the correct pronunciation of letters that are commonly mispronounced.
- Make the entire class repeat the Hadith 3 times with the translation.
- Very simply explain the meaning of the Hadith. If it is something that can be practically demonstrated immediately, then do so. For example the Hadith *"Assalaamu qablal kalaami"* has just been taught. Ask Ahmed to go across the class, meet Yusuf and ask him how he is feeling. Ahmed who has understood the lesson goes to Yusuf and first makes salaam before speaking to him. Praise Ahmed for making salaam first. If he did not make salaam first, ask the class: "What did Ahmed

do wrong?" Make a second child do the same. The same kind of demonstration can be done for various other Ahaadeeth, such as the Ahaadeeth relating to taking care of the Qur-aan, The Best Zikr, Backbiting, Truthfulness, etc.

4.   Commitment

After the above has been done, ask the class: "Who is going to always make salaam first before talking?" After they have put their hands up, praise them and encourage them with a few words. For example, tell them: "Allah سُبْحَانَهُوَتَعَالَى and our beloved Rasulullah صَلَّىٱللَّهُعَلَيْهِوَسَلَّم will be very pleased with us if we practice on these sunnats/Hadith."

5.   Follow up

Do a follow up during the "quick revision" the next day. Enquire who practiced upon the Hadith that was taught the previous day. Praise those who had practiced on it, and encourage those who had not.

There is no pupil activity included in this kitaab. A standard worksheet which includes the following questions should be used at the end of each lesson:

- What is the wording of the Hadith?
- What is the meaning of the Hadith?
- What are the lessons learnt from the Hadith?
- What is the story you learnt from this Hadith?
- How does this Hadith affect you and your fellow Muslims?
- To what extent are you able to practice on this Hadith?

Grade One

SALAAM

قَالَ رَسُوْلُ اللهِ صَلَّى اللهُ عَلَيْهِ وَسَلَّمَ

اَلسَّلَامُ قَبْلَ الْكَلَامِ

Say *Assalaamu alykum* before you begin speaking.

[Tirmizi]

Lessons Learnt

1. Whenever we meet another Muslim we should greet him/her with the words *Assalaamu alykum warahmatullahi wabarakaatuhu*.

2. The word '*Assalaamu alykum*' means "May peace be on you."

3. If we greet with SALAAM, we will be making dua for one another.

4. We should not say "Hi! Hello, Good day or Good morning" as these are not Islamic greetings.

5. We should always be the first to greet. The person, who greets first, gets more reward and it will protect him/her from having pride.

Story 1

Hadhrat Abdullah رَضِىَاللّٰهُعَنْهُ was the son of Hadhrat Umar رَضِىَاللّٰهُعَنْهُ. He had seen Rasulullah صَلَّىاللّٰهُعَلَيْهِوَسَلَّمَ greeting everybody, old and young, rich and poor. Rasulullah صَلَّىاللّٰهُعَلَيْهِوَسَلَّمَ also greeted children.

Hadhrat Abdullah رَضِىَاللّٰهُعَنْهُ loved Rasulullah صَلَّىاللّٰهُعَلَيْهِوَسَلَّمَ so he tried to copy him in making salaam. He made it a habit to pass through the market only to greet people. He greeted everybody he met, the shopkeepers, the passers-by and the children.

One day someone asked him, "You come daily to the shops but you never buy or sell anything. You don't even stop to speak to anyone. Why then do you come to the market?"

Hadhrat Abdullah رَضِىَاللّٰهُعَنْهُ replied, "I come to the market only to make salaam to the people."

Hadith Two

TRUTHFULNESS

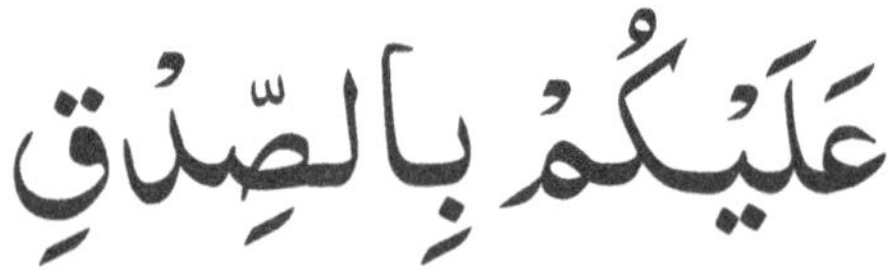

قَالَ رَسُوْلُ اللهِ صَلَّى اللهُ عَلَيْهِ وَسَلَّمَ

عَلَيْكُمْ بِالصِّدْقِ

Be truthful.

[Muslim]

Lessons Learnt

1. A Muslim must always speak the truth.

2. Allah سُبْحَانَهُوَتَعَالَى loves those who speak the truth.

3. Allah سُبْحَانَهُوَتَعَالَى will take care of those people who always speak the truth.

4. A person who is truthful will enter Jannah.

5. A liar will be punished by Allah سُبْحَانَهُوَتَعَالَى.

Hadhrat Abdul Qadir Jilaani رَحِمَهُ اللهُ was a very great saint. When he was a young boy, he decided to go to Baghdad to learn Islamic knowledge. Before leaving, his mother gave him 40 gold coins and sewed them in an inside pocket. She then told him never to speak a lie. He promised his mother that he will obey her and not speak a lie.

In those days there were no cars, trains or planes. People used to travel in groups forming a caravan. Shaikh Abdul Qadir رَحِمَهُ اللهُ also joined a caravan going to Baghdad.

On the way, a gang of robbers attacked the caravan and started stealing. A robber came to Shaikh Abdul Qadir رَحِمَهُ اللهُ and asked if he had any money. He replied that he had 40 gold coins. The robber thought that he was joking so he left him alone.

After a while, another robber came and asked Shaikh Abdul Qadir رَحِمَهُ اللهُ if he had any money. Again he replied that he had 40 gold coins. The robber didn't believe him because he looked like he was poor. The second robber also left him alone. The news of this young boy reached the leader of the robbers. The leader told them to bring the young boy to him.

When Shaikh Abdul Qadir رَحِمَهُ اللهُ was brought, the leader of the robbers asked him if he had any money. Shaikh Abdul Qadir رَحِمَهُ اللهُ replied that he had 40 gold coins with him. The leader of the robbers asked, "Where is it?" "Sewn in an inside pocket." he replied. The leader told one of the robbers to search the young boy. When the robber searched him, he found the 40 gold coins which were hidden in an inside pocket. On seeing this, all the robbers were surprised. The leader said, "You know we are robbers and we steal money from people. Your money was safely hidden. If you lied to us that you did not have any money, we would have believed you and your money would have been safe. What made you speak the truth and show us your money?"

Shaikh Abdul Qadir رَحِمَهُ اللّٰه replied, "Before I left home, my mother told me never to speak a lie. Therefore I will not disobey my mother, not even for the sake of 40 gold coins." The words of this young boy greatly affected the leader of the robbers who said, "This boy has obeyed his mother whereas I have disobeyed Allah سُبْحَانَهُ وَتَعَالَى for my whole life. I make *taubah* for my sins and promise not to trouble anyone for the rest of my life." The other robbers also made *taubah* and returned all the money to the people. They then lived their lives obeying Allah سُبْحَانَهُ وَتَعَالَى and became His close friends.

TAKING CARE OF THE QUR-AAN

قَالَ رَسُوْلُ اللهِ صَلَّى اللهُ عَلَيْهِ وَسَلَّمَ

تَعَاهَدُوا الْقُرْاٰنَ

Take good care of the Qur-aan.

[Bukhaari]

Lessons Learnt

1. Since the Qur-aan is the book of Allah سُبْحَانَهُ وَتَعَالَى, we must always show respect to it.

2. Always make wudhu before touching the Qur-aan.

3. Place the Qur-aan on a clean and high place.

4. Always hold it in your right hand close to your heart.

5. Do not face your back or stretch your feet towards the Qur-aan.

6. Do not put your Qur-aan in your school bag.

Story 3

There was a man who was not a good Muslim, but he had great respect for the Qur-aan, and its pages. While walking, he found a page of the Qur-aan on the floor. He picked it up, kissed it, dusted the sand off and placed it on a high shelf with respect. Allah سُبْحَانَهُ وَتَعَالَى loved this action and forgave him.

Story 4

A pious person used to stay in Madinah Munawwarah. He passed away and was buried in Jannatul Baqi' (the graveyard in Madinah). The practice in Makkah Mukarramah and Madinah Munawwarah is that a few months after they bury anybody, they dig up the same grave and bury someone else in it because of the large number of people that pass away there. A few months later, they dug up the grave of this pious person and found that his body was still fresh.

A few months later, they once again dug up the grave of this pious person and again found his body fresh. They closed up the grave and put a mark on it saying that this grave would not be dug up again.

They went to the son of the pious man and asked, "What action of your father was so liked by Allah سُبْحَانَهُ وَتَعَالَى that Allah سُبْحَانَهُ وَتَعَالَى did not allow his body to rot?" The son replied, "Allah سُبْحَانَهُ وَتَعَالَى knows best. I feel that it was the respect that he had for the Qur-aan Shareef. He would not stretch his legs in the direction of a Haafiz. He would say, '(The haafiz) has the Qur-aan in his chest.'"

Hadith Four

SPYING

Do not spy.

[Bukhaari]

Lessons Learnt

1. A Muslim does not spy on other people. Spying is an evil habit.

2. Spying creates hatred because you are interfering in another person's life.

3. By spying you will be finding fault with another Muslim whereas finding faults of others is haraam.

4. We should hide each others faults.

5. Do not spy into another person's home or room intentionally.

Story 5

Once, when Rasulullah ﷺ was walking with a group of Sahaabah رَضِيَ اللهُ عَنْهُمْ they passed by two graves. Rasulullah ﷺ said, "The two people buried in these graves are being punished. One is being punished <u>because of spying / carrying tales</u> and the other is being punished because of not being careful about the splashes of urine."

Story 6

Once, a person was selling a slave. Someone came and bought the slave. Before selling him, the seller told the buyer that the slave has the fault of carrying tales. The buyer did not worry about it and still bought the slave. He took the slave home and gave him work to do. After working for a few days, the slave came to the wife of the master and told her that her husband didn't love her anymore and was planning to marry another lady.

The wife said in shock, "What are you saying?" The slave said, "I am telling the truth. However, I have a plan which, if you carry out, will make him love you more than anyone else." The master's wife said, "Tell me this plan." The slave said, "When your husband sleeps at night, shave off a few hairs from under his beard. And give me this hair. I will use it to make him really love you."

The slave then went to the master and said, "It seems that your wife is interested in someone else and wishes to kill you." The master said in surprise, "That cannot be possible." The slave said, "Test it out yourself. Tonight pretend to be asleep and see what happens."

That night, the wife took a blade and stretched her hand forward to shave some hair from behind his beard. As she put her hand forward, the master caught her hand and killed her with the same razor. The wife's family heard about it and killed the husband. In turn the husband's family heard about this and began fighting with the wife's family. This fight lasted for many years. This was all because of the evil of carrying tales.

FEEDING THE HUNGRY

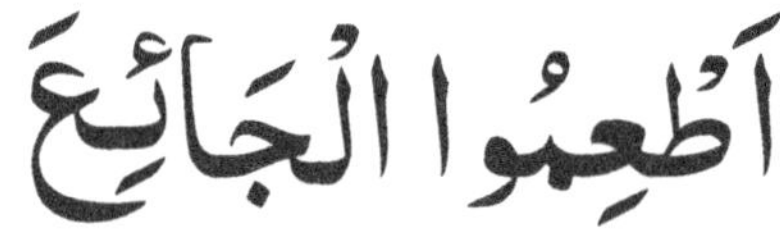

قَالَ رَسُوْلُ اللهِ صَلَّى اللهُ عَلَيْهِ وَسَلَّمَ

أَطْعِمُوا الْجَائِعَ

Feed the hungry.

[Bukhaari]

Lessons Learnt

1. To feed the poor and hungry is an action that will be greatly rewarded by Allah سُبْحَانَهُ وَتَعَالَى.

2. A Muslim should not fill his stomach whilst his neighbour remains hungry.

3. We should always serve the poor and needy.

4. Allah سُبْحَانَهُ وَتَعَالَى loves those who take care of the poor and needy.

Hadhrat Hasan رَضِىَاللهُعَنهُ and Hadhrat Husain رَضِىَاللهُعَنهُ once fell very ill. Hadhrat Ali رَضِىَاللهُعَنهُ and Hadhrat Faatimah رَضِىَاللهُعَنها took a vow that if their sons recovered, they would fast for three days to show thanks to Allah Ta'ala. Allah restored their children's health and they started fasting. There was no food in the house, or any money to buy food for Sehri or Iftaar. They began fasting while they were starving. In the morning, Hadhrat Ali رَضِىَاللهُعَنهُ went to a Jew, and brought a bale of wool to spin into yarn, in return for which the Jew promised to give them some barley as wages. On the first day of fasting, Faatimah رَضِىَاللهُعَنها spun one third of the bale of wool, and the Jew gave them some barley. She ground the barley and baked five small loaves of bread, one each for Ali, Faatimah, Hasan, Husain and Fidhah رَضِىَاللهُعَنهم, the slave-maid.

When the fast was completed and Ali رَضِىَاللهُعَنهُ came back from the Masjid after performing the Maghrib Salaah in jamaat with Rasulullah صَلَّىَاللهُعَلَيهِوَسَلَّم, the family sat down for supper, all tired from the days' work and hungry. As soon as Ali رَضِىَاللهُعَنهُ took a piece of bread in his hand, he heard the voice of a beggar from outside, saying. "O family of Rasulullah صَلَّىَاللهُعَلَيهِوَسَلَّم, I am a very poor beggar. Please give me something to eat. May Allah Ta'ala feed you with the delicious food of Jannah!" Ali رَضِىَاللهُعَنهُ did not put the piece of bread into his mouth and spoke to Faatimah رَضِىَاللهُعَنها, who said that all the bread should be given to the beggar. So, they gave all five loaves to the beggar and the entire family remained without any food. They also fasted the following day and, on that day Faatimah رَضِىَاللهُعَنها spun more of the wool, for which the Jew gave them some barley which she ground into flour and again baked into five loaves of bread. That evening, when Ali رَضِىَاللهُعَنهُ came back from the Masjid, after performing the Maghrib Salaah, in Jamaat with Rasulullah صَلَّىَاللهُعَلَيهِوَسَلَّم, and the family sat down to have supper there came the voice of an orphan from outside, who asked for food and said that he was very poor and all alone in this world. They once again gave all five loaves of bread to the orphan child and went to bed after breaking their fast with water. They also fasted on the third day too, and Faatima رَضِىَاللّٰهُعَنْهَا had spun the remaining wool into yarn, for which the Jew gave them some barley which she ground into flour and baked into five loaves of bread. On that day when they sat down for supper, there came from outside, the voice of a prisoner, who asked for help and said that he was in great difficulty. So they gave him all five loaves of bread and they themselves again went to bed without any food.

On the fourth day, they were not fasting, but had absolutely nothing to eat. Hadhrat Ali رَضِىَاللّٰهُعَنْهُ took Hadhrat Hasan رَضِىَاللّٰهُعَنْهُ and Hadhrat Husain رَضِىَاللّٰهُعَنْهُ to meet Rasulullah صَلَّىاللّٰهُعَلَيْهِوَسَلَّم. They could hardly walk because they had become too weak due to starving for three days. Rasulullah صَلَّىاللّٰهُعَلَيْهِوَسَلَّم said to them, "It hurts me to see you suffering from hunger and misery. Let us go to Faatimah." Rasulullah صَلَّىاللّٰهُعَلَيْهِوَسَلَّم then went to Hadhrat Faatimah رَضِىَاللّٰهُعَنْهَا, and saw that she was performing Nafl Salaah. Her eyes had sunk in, and her belly had come close to her back due to severe starvation. Rasulullah صَلَّىاللّٰهُعَلَيْهِوَسَلَّم hugged his daughter and made dua for Allah's mercy to come to her and her family. At this, Jibraa-eel عَلَيْهِالسَّلَام came with the following verse of the Holy Qur-aan:

$$ \text{وَيُطْعِمُونَ الطَّعَامَ عَلَىٰ حُبِّهِ مِسْكِينًا وَّيَتِيمًا وَّأَسِيرًا ﴿٨﴾} $$

And they feed the needy, the orphan and the prisoner out of love
for Him. (Surah ad-Dahr:8)

Jibraeel عَلَيْهِالسَّلَام congratulated them, saying that Allah was pleased with them.

When Rasulullah صَلَّىاللّٰهُعَلَيْهِوَسَلَّم heard of this, he was filled with joy and pleased with his daughter. Indeed! Allah سُبْحَانَهُوَتَعَالَى was also pleased with this act of kindness.

Grade Two

CLEANLINESS

قَالَ رَسُوْلُ اللهِ صَلَّى اللهُ عَلَيْهِ وَسَلَّمَ

اَلطُّهُوْرُ شَطْرُ الْاِيْمَانِ

Cleanliness is half of Imaan (faith).

[Muslim]

Lessons Learnt

1. Cleanliness is a very important part of Islam.

2. We should be clean and pure at all times.

3. Make istinjaa, wudhu and ghusal thoroughly.

4. Our bodies, clothes, books, classrooms, homes, yards, etc. must be kept clean, neat and tidy at all times.

5. Angels remain with a person who is clean and pure at all times.

Story 8

Once, when Rasulullah ﷺ was walking with a group of Sahabah رَضِيَ اللهُ عَنْهُم, they passed by two graves. Rasulullah ﷺ said, "The two people buried in these graves are being punished. One is being punished for spying and the other is being punished for <u>not being careful about the splashes of urine</u>."

Story 9

A Muslim student once went to London to study. He found a place to stay at a house where other students were also staying. This house was owned by an English woman.

One day this woman asked the Muslim student, "Do you think that I do not know how to wash clothes?" "Why do you ask that?" asked the student. "I am quite sure that you know how to wash clothes." The woman said, "Then why do you wash your clothes before giving it to me for washing?" The student replied, "I do not wash my clothes before giving it to you. If I did wash my clothes, I wouldn't have given it to you." "Then why don't I find marks, stains and bad smells on your pants whereas I find them on the pants of the other boys?" asked the woman.

The student explained, "Madam, I am a Muslim. My religion teaches me to be clean. If a drop of urine comes onto my pants, I have to immediately wash it off. I am not allowed to perform Salaah until I do so." The woman asked, "Does your religion teach you about cleanliness as well?" The student replied, "Yes, our

Prophet ﷺ has taught us such things. He taught us to remember Allah ﷻ at all times. He taught us duas for all occasions."

The woman found this to be wonderful. Thereafter she began to carefully watch the behaviour, manners and habits of the Muslim student and she began to like Islam. She would ask him questions about Islam until one day the truth of Islam filled her heart and she became a Muslim. Not only did she accept Islam but she also invited many people of her family who accepted Islam.

SALAAH

قَالَ رَسُوْلُ اللهِ صَلَّى اللهُ عَلَيْهِ وَسَلَّمَ

اَلصَّلٰوةُ عِمَادُ الدِّيْنِ

Salaah is a pillar of Deen.

[Shu'bul Imaan]

Lessons Learnt

1. Salaah is the most important form of Ibaadah (worship)

2. When we perform our Salaah, we are showing our obedience to our creator.

3. Salaah is the key to Jannah.

4. The first question we will be asked on the day of Qiyaamah will be about Salaah.

5. Reading our Salaah will protect us from evil and sins.

Story 10

Once, a woman died. Her brother was at the graveside when she was buried. By mistake his bag fell inside the grave without anyone noticing. When he came home he realised what had happened. He needed the bag because he had some important papers in it. He decided to secretly go and dig up the grave. When he dug the grave up, he saw that it was full of fire and his sister was being punished. This made him very sad. He went home and told his mother what he had seen. He asked her if she knew why his sister was being punished. His mother replied that it was probably because **she used to delay her salaah and perform it after the time of salaah had passed**.

Story 11

A great saint once said, "Have your needs fulfilled by Allah سُبْحَانَهُوَتَعَالَى by reading Salaah. In the past, when people were affected by a calamity, they would hurry and perform Salaah."

There was once a porter (a person who carries and transports goods for people) who was well known for his honesty. People used to give him their money and other valuables to take to different places. Once he was taking some goods to a certain place when he met a man on the way who asked him where he was going. He informed the man. The man asked the porter to give him a lift on his mule. The porter made place for the man on his mule and they continued on their journey.

When they came to a crossroad (where one road branches off into two or more roads), the man asked the porter, "Which road will you take?" "The main road," said the porter. The man said, "No, take the other road. It is shorter and there is plenty of grass on the way for the mule to feed on. I have travelled on it often so I know this road." The porter believed him. After a distance, the road ended. There were many dead bodies lying about. The man jumped off the mule and pulled out a knife with the intention of killing the porter. The porter said, "Take the mule and the goods but don't kill me." The man insisted on killing the porter. The porter asked the man for a chance to perform two rakaats Salaah. The man said, "You can do as you please. All these dead people asked for the same thing but their Salaah did not help them." The porter began his Salaah but could not think of anything to read after Surah Faatihah. Meanwhile the man was getting impatient and told the porter to hurry up. Suddenly the following aayah of the Qur-aan came to the mind of the porter:

اَمَّنْ يُّجِيْبُ الْمُضْطَرَّ اِذَا دَعَاهُ وَ يَكْشِفُ السُّوْءَ

'Who is The One who answers the call of the one who is wronged and removes the evil ....'

The porter recited this verse and tears came to his eyes when suddenly a horseman appeared. He was wearing a shining helmet and carried a spear in his hand. He stabbed the rogue with the spear and killed him. A flame of fire rose from the spot where the dead body fell.

The porter went into sajdah and thanked Allah ﷻ for saving

him. He quickly completed his Salaah, ran towards the horseman and asked him who he was. The horseman replied, "I am a slave of The One Allah who answers the call of the person who is wronged (He was an angel). You are now safe and you may go wherever you please." The horseman then rode away and disappeared.

THE BEST ZIKR

قَالَ رَسُوْلُ اللهِ صَلَّى اللهُ عَلَيْهِ وَسَلَّمَ

اَفْضَلُ الذِّكْرِ لَاۤ اِلٰهَ اِلَّا اللهُ

The best type of Zikr is "**Laa ilaha illallah**".

[Tirmizi]

Lessons Learnt

1. Zikr means to remember or think of Allah سُبْحَانَهُ وَتَعَالَى.

2. A person who remembers Allah سُبْحَانَهُ وَتَعَالَى, Allah سُبْحَانَهُ وَتَعَالَى remembers him.

3. By making Zikr, our hearts will be cleansed of all evil qualities.

4. A person who recites **laa ilaha illallah** 100 times daily, his face will shine like the full moon on the day of Qiyaamah.

5. A person who makes the Zikr of Allah سُبْحَانَهُ وَتَعَالَى is like a living person, whilst a person who does not make Zikr is like a dead person (spiritually).

Story 12

Once, Hadhrat Moosa عَلَيْهِ السَّلَام asked Allah سُبْحَانَهُ وَتَعَالَى to teach him a special type of Zikr. Allah سُبْحَانَهُ وَتَعَالَى told him to read **laa ilaha illallah**. Hadhrat Moosa عَلَيْهِ السَّلَام said that this Zikr is read by everybody. Allah سُبْحَانَهُ وَتَعَالَى again told him to read **laa ilaha illallah**. Hadhrat Moosa عَلَيْهِ السَّلَام replied that he wanted a Zikr that was for him only. Allah سُبْحَانَهُ وَتَعَالَى said, "O Moosa عَلَيْهِ السَّلَام, if the seven skies and the seven earths were placed on one side of the scale and the kalimah **laa ilaha illallah** was placed on the other side, the kalimah will be heavier."

Story 13

Abu Yazeed Qurtubi رَحْمَةُ اللهِ writes, "I learnt that the person who reads

لَا اِلٰهَ اِلَّا الله

seventy thousand times will be saved from the fire of Jahannam, I completed this number once for my wife and few times for myself.

There used to live near us a young man who was known to be blessed with the power of kashf (Allah سُبْحَانَهُ وَتَعَالَى sometimes allows him to see certain things of the unseen like what is happening in someone's grave, Jannat, Jahannam, etc.) but I hesitated to believe it.

Once, this young man was eating with us when he suddenly shouted and said, "I see my mother burning in the fire of Jahannam." When I saw how worried he was, I thought of giving one of my complete seventy thousand zikrs of the Kalimah for his mother. I quietly did so in my heart without telling anybody about it. As soon as I did this, the young man became happy and said, "O Uncle, my mother has been saved from the punishment of Jahannam." I learnt two things from this story: Firstly, the reward of reading the Kalimah seventy thousand times was proved by actual experience, and secondly, it showed that the young man was really blessed with the power of kashf."

Hadith Nine

HELPING OTHERS

قَالَ رَسُوْلُ اللهِ صَلَّى اللهُ عَلَيْهِ وَسَلَّمَ

خَيْرُ النَّاسِ اَنْفَعُهُمْ لِلنَّاسِ

The best person is one who benefits other people.

[Kanzul Ummaal]

Lessons Learnt

1. We should always help others.

2. We must sacrifice ourselves and our things to help others.

3. When we help others they will love us.

4. They will make dua for us and Allah سُبْحَانَهُ وَتَعَالَى will help us.

Hadhrat Umar ﷺ was a great ruler. He used to walk around the city at night so that he would know the condition of the people and help them. His wish to help people stopped him from sleeping at night. One night he went outside Madinah Munawwarah. He saw a tent outside which a very worried man was sitting. He also heard a groaning sound coming from inside the tent. Hadhrat Umar ﷺ asked him what was happening inside the tent. The man replied that he was a traveller and inside the tent was his wife who was about to have a child. He also said that he had no food or money and he did not know anyone who could help him.

Hadhrat Umar ﷺ immediately ran home and said to his wife, "O my wife! Allah ﷻ has given us a chance to earn great sawaab. Are you ready for it?" He then explained to her what had happened. She readily agreed. Hadhrat Umar ﷺ took some flour and butter and his wife took the things that are needed when a child is to be born. They returned quickly to the tent. Hadhrat Umar ﷺ sat with the man and prepared some food while his wife went inside the tent and served as a nurse. After a little while, Hadhrat Umar's ﷺ wife called out, "O Ameerul Mumineen! Give your friend the good news of a boy." It was then that the man came to know that he was sitting with the leader of the Muslims. He became embarrassed because Hadhrat Umar ﷺ was serving him. Hadhrat Umar ﷺ said, "Don't worry. The work of a leader is to serve." They then gave him some food and money and returned home.

SWEARING

قَالَ رَسُوْلُ اللهِ صَلَّى اللهُ عَلَيْهِ وَسَلَّمَ

سِبَابُ الْمُسْلِمِ فُسُوْقٌ

Swearing a Muslim is a major sin.

[Bukhaari]

Lessons Learnt

1. Swearing is an evil habit.

2. A person who swears loses his respect.

3. If you swear others they will swear you in return.

4. Swearing will create more problems instead of solving the problem.

Once, a man began to swear Hadhrat Abu Bakr رَضِيَ اللهُ عَنْهُ whilst Rasulullah صَلَّى اللهُ عَلَيْهِ وَسَلَّمَ was also there. Hadhrat Abu Bakr رَضِيَ اللهُ عَنْهُ remained silent. The man continued to swear him but Abu Bakr رَضِيَ اللهُ عَنْهُ continued to remain silent. After some time, Hadhrat Abu Bakr رَضِيَ اللهُ عَنْهُ said something to him. When he did this, Rasulullah صَلَّى اللهُ عَلَيْهِ وَسَلَّمَ got up and began to walk away. Hadhrat Abu Bakr رَضِيَ اللهُ عَنْهُ immediately got up and went after Rasulullah صَلَّى اللهُ عَلَيْهِ وَسَلَّمَ. He asked Rasulullah صَلَّى اللهُ عَلَيْهِ وَسَلَّمَ the reason for going away. Rasulullah صَلَّى اللهُ عَلَيْهِ وَسَلَّمَ replied, "As long as you remained silent, Allah سُبْحَانَهُ وَتَعَالَى sent an angel to reply to him on your behalf. When you said something in revenge, the angel went away and shaytaan came. I, therefore, went away."

Grade Three

JANNAH LIES BENEATH THE FEET OF THE MOTHER

قَالَ رَسُوْلُ اللهِ صَلَّى اللهُ عَلَيْهِ وَسَلَّمَ

اَلْجَنَّةُ تَحْتَ اَقْدَامِ الْاُمَّهَاتِ

Jannah is under the feet of the mothers.

[Kanzul Ummaal]

Lessons Learnt

1. Always obey your parents.
2. Never trouble them in anyway.
3. Speak to them with kindness and love.
4. Do not even say "Aakh! or Oof! to them.
5. When they are old and weak and they need you then you must serve them well.
6. Make this dua for them;

رَبِّ ارْحَمْهُمَا كَمَا رَبَّيَانِيْ صَغِيْرًا

"O Allah, Show mercy to my parents like how they showed mercy to me when I was small."

Alqamah رَضِيَ ٱللَّهُ عَنْهُ was a young Sahaabi who was very generous and used to work hard for Deen. Suddenly he became very sick. Rasulullah صَلَّى ٱللَّهُ عَلَيْهِ وَسَلَّمَ came to know of his sickness and sent Hadhrat Bilaal رَضِيَ ٱللَّهُ عَنْهُ to check on him. When Hadhrat Bilaal رَضِيَ ٱللَّهُ عَنْهُ came to Alqamah's رَضِيَ ٱللَّهُ عَنْهُ house, he saw that Alqamah رَضِيَ ٱللَّهُ عَنْهُ was about to pass away. He tried to make him read the kalimah, but Alqamah رَضِيَ ٱللَّهُ عَنْهُ was unable to read it. Rasulullah صَلَّى ٱللَّهُ عَلَيْهِ وَسَلَّمَ was told of this.

Rasulullah صَلَّى ٱللَّهُ عَلَيْهِ وَسَلَّمَ asked if Alqamah's رَضِيَ ٱللَّهُ عَنْهُ parents were alive. The Sahaabah replied that only his mother was alive and she was very old. Rasulullah صَلَّى ٱللَّهُ عَلَيْهِ وَسَلَّمَ sent Hadhrat Bilaal رَضِيَ ٱللَّهُ عَنْهُ to ask her if she could come to Rasulullah صَلَّى ٱللَّهُ عَلَيْهِ وَسَلَّمَ or else he would come to her. She replied, "May my life be sacrificed for Rasulullah صَلَّى ٱللَّهُ عَلَيْهِ وَسَلَّمَ! I will go to him." She used a walking stick and went to Rasulullah صَلَّى ٱللَّهُ عَلَيْهِ وَسَلَّمَ. She made salaam and sat down. Rasulullah صَلَّى ٱللَّهُ عَلَيْهِ وَسَلَّمَ replied to her salaam and said, "I am now going to ask you some questions. Please answer them truthfully otherwise I will be informed through *wahi* if you lie."

Rasulullah صَلَّى ٱللَّهُ عَلَيْهِ وَسَلَّمَ then asked, "What kind of a person is Alqamah رَضِيَ ٱللَّهُ عَنْهُ?" She replied, "He performs lots of salaah, keeps lots of fasts and is very generous." Rasulullah صَلَّى ٱللَّهُ عَلَيْهِ وَسَلَّمَ asked, "How is he with you?" She replied that she was angry with him. When Rasulullah صَلَّى ٱللَّهُ عَلَيْهِ وَسَلَّمَ asked her why, she said, "He chooses his wife over me." Rasulullah صَلَّى ٱللَّهُ عَلَيْهِ وَسَلَّمَ told her that the anger of his mother is not allowing him to read the kalimah.

Thereafter, Rasulullah ﷺ told Hadhrat Bilaal رَضِيَ اللهُ عَنْهُ to get some wood and start a fire in which Alqamah رَضِيَ اللهُ عَنْهُ would be thrown. His mother asked in shock, "Will you burn my son in front of me? I cannot allow this." Rasulullah ﷺ said, "The fire of Allah سُبْحَانَهُ وَتَعَالَى is much worse than this and lasts forever. If you want Allah سُبْحَانَهُ وَتَعَالَى to forgive him then be pleased with him. I take an oath in the name of Allah سُبْحَانَهُ وَتَعَالَى that without pleasing you, his salaah and other good deeds will not help him." She immediately said, "O Prophet of Allah! I make you witness that I am pleased with my son Alqamah رَضِيَ اللهُ عَنْهُ."

Rasulullah ﷺ then told Hadhrat Bilaal رَضِيَ اللهُ عَنْهُ to go and see Alqamah's رَضِيَ اللهُ عَنْهُ condition. When Hadhrat Bilaal رَضِيَ اللهُ عَنْهُ entered the house, he heard Hadhrat Alqamah رَضِيَ اللهُ عَنْهُ reading the kalimah loudly and soon thereafter he passed away.

MAKING YOUR FATHER ANGRY

قَالَ رَسُوْلُ اللهِ صَلَّى اللهُ عَلَيْهِ وَسَلَّمَ

سَخَطُ الرَّبِّ فِيْ سَخَطِ الْوَالِدِ

Allah سُبْحَانَهُ وَتَعَالَى is angry with a person whose father is angry with him. [Mustadrak Haakim]

Lessons Learnt

1. It is waajib (compulsory) to obey your father in whatever he commands you to do. (so long as it is permissible)

2. Nabi صَلَّى اللَّهُ عَلَيْهِ وَسَلَّم said: "There are three rights of a father: 1. Don't call him by his name. 2. Don't walk in front of him. 3. Don't sit down before he sits.

3. Always be good and kind to your father's friends. Whenever you see them, go and greet them.

4. Nabi صَلَّى اللَّهُ عَلَيْهِ وَسَلَّم has said that you and your wealth belong to your father.

HATRED

Do not hate one another.

[Bukhaari]

Lessons Learnt

1. To hate another person is a major sin.

2. As Muslims we should love each other.

3. We must always keep our hearts clean.

4. If we had a problem or a fight, we should be the first to ask for forgiveness.

Hadhrat Anas رَضِىَ اللهُ عَنْهُ says, "Once we were sitting with Rasulullah صَلَّى اللهُ عَلَيْهِ وَسَلَّمَ when he said, 'Very soon a person from Jannah will enter.' A man from the Ansaar entered with his shoes in his left hand and water dripping from his beard (showing that he had just made wudhu). The next day Rasulullah صَلَّى اللهُ عَلَيْهِ وَسَلَّمَ said the same thing and the same man entered with his shoes in his left hand and water dripping from his beard. On the third day the same thing happened.

When Rasulullah صَلَّى اللهُ عَلَيْهِ وَسَلَّمَ went away, Hadhrat Abdullah bin Umar رَضِىَ اللهُ عَنْهُ went up to that man and said, 'I had an argument with my father and took an oath that I will not stay at home for three days. Please allow me to stay with you for three days.' Hadhrat Abdullah bin Umar رَضِىَ اللهُ عَنْهُ spent three nights with that Sahaabi and did not see him do any extra ibaadah. After three days he said to that Sahaabi, 'I did not have any argument with my father. I wanted to see what special action you are doing that made Rasulullah صَلَّى اللهُ عَلَيْهِ وَسَلَّمَ say that you are a man of Jannah. Thus I only made an excuse to come and stay with you. Now after staying with you, I don't see anything special.'

The Sahaabi said, 'I don't do anything special. However, I don't have hatred or jealousy for any Muslim.' Hadhrat Abdullah رَضِىَ اللهُ عَنْهُ then said, 'This must be the quality that makes you a Jannati.'"

BACKBITING

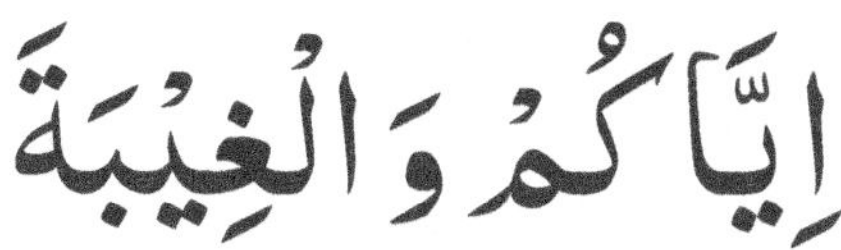

Save yourself from backbiting.

[Kanzul Ummaal]

Lessons Learnt

1. Backbiting means to say such things about someone in his absence which if he happens to hear he will dislike.

2. If what is said about him is true then this is gheebah and if not, then it is slander, which is worse than backbiting.

3. Backbiting creates disunity, fighting, hatred, jealousy, etc.

4. Backbiting is like eating someone's dead flesh.

5. We are giving all our good deeds away to that person whom we speak ill of.

Rasulullah ﷺ once commanded the people to fast and said to them that none of them should break their fast until he gives them permission. When the night set in, a person came to Rasulullah ﷺ and said, "O Rasulullah ﷺ, please allow me to break my fast." Rasulullah ﷺ allowed him. Another person came for permission and was also allowed to break his fast. A third person came and said, "O Rasulullah ﷺ, there are two women who are finding the fast very difficult. They are feeling shy to ask you for permission to break their fast. Please give them permission." Rasulullah ﷺ turned away from him. He asked a second time but again Rasulullah ﷺ turned away from him. When he asked for the third time, Rasulullah ﷺ turned away from him and said, "They did not fast. They were eating the flesh of people during the day (they were speaking bad of others). Go and tell them to vomit." This man went and told those two women to vomit. When they vomited, blood and pieces of flesh came out. He returned and told Rasulullah ﷺ of what happened. Rasulullah ﷺ said, "If that blood and flesh remained in their stomachs, they would have entered the fire of Jahannam."

VISITING THE SICK

قَالَ رَسُوْلُ اللهِ صَلَّى اللهُ عَلَيْهِ وَسَلَّمَ

Visit the sick.

[Bukhaari]

Lessons Learnt

1. Visiting the sick is a very good action which has great rewards.

2. Angels make dua for a person who visit the sick.

3. Give the sick person hope that he will soon get better.

4. Keep your visit short when visiting the sick.

5. Ask the sick person to make dua for you as his dua is accepted.

6. Allah سُبْحَانَهُ وَتَعَالَى builds a palace in Jannah for a person who visits the sick.

7. 70 000 angels make dua for a person who visits the sick.

Story 19

Hadhrat Sirri Siqti رَحْمَةُٱللّٰه said, "Once, I had fallen ill and was suffering with diarrhoea (running stomach). Some people had come to visit me. They sat for so long that I thought that they were going to stay for the whole day. Their long stay caused me great difficulty because, with them around, it was difficult for me to go to the toilet every now and again. When they were leaving, they asked me to make dua for them. I raised my hands saying, 'O Allah! Teach them the correct way of visiting the sick'."

Story 20

Once, Allah سُبْحَانَهُوَتَعَالَى told Hadhrat Moosa عَلَيْهِٱلسَّلَام, "O Moosa! I am sick and you are not coming to visit me." Hadhrat Moosa عَلَيْهِٱلسَّلَام asked, "O Allah! You are The Greatest. You do not get sick. What do you mean by saying that you are sick and I did not come to visit you?"

Allah سُبْحَانَهُوَتَعَالَى replied, "O Moosa! A certain Muslim is sick. Go and visit him because when you will visit him, you will come close to Me. If you visit the sick, you will get lots of sawaab. Visit the sick person even if he is your enemy as this visit could make him your friend. Even if he does not become your friend, at least he will stop fighting with you."

SEEKING KNOWLEDGE

قَالَ رَسُوْلُ اللهِ صَلَّى اللهُ عَلَيْهِ وَسَلَّمَ

طَلَبُ الْعِلْمِ فَرِيْضَةٌ عَلَى كُلِّ مُسْلِمٍ

Seeking knowledge is the compulsory duty of every Muslim.

[Ibn Majah]

Lessons Learnt

1. Ilm or Knowledge of Islam is the greatest treasure that any person can get.
2. Ignorance (having no knowledge) of Islam is the worst poverty.
3. Without ilm, a person will never understand his purpose of life nor will he be able to practice his Deen.
4. When a person seeks the knowledge of Deen, angels accompany him and he is rewarded for every step he takes towards the place of learning.
5. A student of Deen is protected from sin when he learns and the mercy of Allah سُبْحَانَهُ وَتَعَالَى rains down on him.
6. We should always try to learn more about our Deen.

Katsir bin Qais رَحِمَهُ ٱللَّهُ says, "I was sitting with Hadhrat Abu Darda رَضِيَ ٱللَّهُ عَنْهُ in a masjid in Damascus when a person came to him and said, 'O Abu Darda رَضِيَ ٱللَّهُ عَنْهُ! I have come all the way from Madinah Munawwarah to learn one Hadith from you because you have heard it directly from Rasulullah صَلَّى ٱللَّهُ عَلَيْهِ وَسَلَّمَ.' Hadhrat Abu Darda رَضِيَ ٱللَّهُ عَنْهُ asked him if he had any other work in Damascus. He replied that he did not have any other work. Hadhrat Abu Darda رَضِيَ ٱللَّهُ عَنْهُ again asked, 'Are you sure you have no other work in Damascus?' He replied, 'I have come here only to learn this Hadith from you.' Hadhrat Abu Darda رَضِيَ ٱللَّهُ عَنْهُ then said, 'Listen! I have heard Rasulullah صَلَّى ٱللَّهُ عَلَيْهِ وَسَلَّمَ saying that Allah سُبْحَانَهُ وَتَعَالَى makes the way to Jannah easy for the person who travels to seek knowledge. The angels spread their wings for him and everything in the heavens and earth, even the fish in the sea, make dua for his forgiveness. The greatness of a person of knowledge over a person involved in 'ibaadat (worshiping Allah), is like the greatness of the moon over the stars. The Ulama are the inheritors of the Ambiyaa عَلَيْهِمُ ٱلسَّلَامُ. The Ambiyaa عَلَيْهِمُ ٱلسَّلَامُ did not leave behind gold and silver. They left behind knowledge. A person who acquires knowledge acquires a great wealth.'"

Hadhrat Abu Darda رَضِيَ ٱللَّهُ عَنْهُ was one of the Sahaabah who had great knowledge. He is known as Hakeemul-Ummah (The very wise person of the ummah).

Hadhrat Anas رَضِيَ اللهُ عَنْهُ says that Rasulullah صَلَّى اللهُ عَلَيْهِ وَسَلَّمَ said, "If you wish to see people who are freed from the fire of Jahannam, then look at the students of Deen. By Allah سُبْحَانَهُ وَتَعَالَى, when a student goes to the door of an 'Aalim with the intention of learning, for every step that he takes he will be given the reward of one years 'ibaadah. Every piece of ground that he steps on makes dua for his forgiveness and day and night the angels announce, 'Here are those whom Allah سُبْحَانَهُ وَتَعَالَى has freed from the fire (of Jahannam).' In this way a palace is built for him in Jannah."

Story 22

Many students were studying Hadith in Madinah Munawwarah by Imaam Maalik رَحِمَهُ اللهُ. One day there was an announcement that an elephant had come into the town. An elephant is a very strange animal to the Arabs. The students heard this announcement and immediately left the lessons and ran out. One of the students, whose name was Yahya, remained seated peacefully. Imaam Maalik رَحِمَهُ اللهُ asked him: "There are no elephants in the country you live in. Why don't you also go to see it?" Yahya replied: "Hadhrat, I left Spain to meet you and learn from you. I did not leave my hometown to see elephants." Imaam Maalik رَحِمَهُ اللهُ was very pleased when he heard this reply and gave him the title; "The most intelligent of the people of Andalus (Spain)."

Grade

Four

SINCERITY

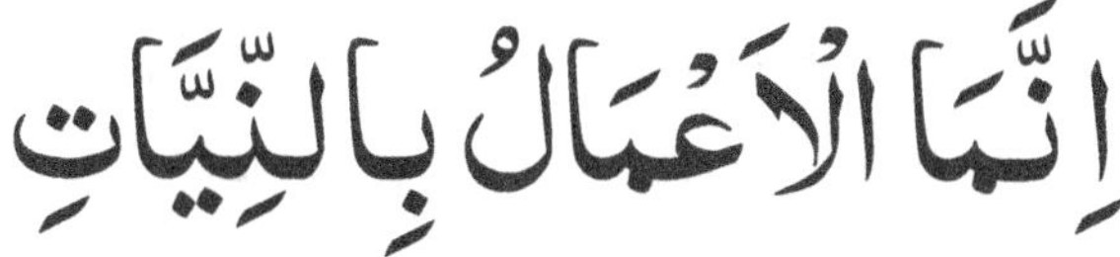

قَالَ رَسُوْلُ اللهِ صَلَّى اللهُ عَلَيْهِ وَسَلَّمَ

اِنَّمَا الْاَعْمَالُ بِالنِّيَّاتِ

Certainly, actions depend on their intentions.

[Bukhaari]

Lessons Learnt

1. The intention we make before doing any action will decide whether we will be rewarded for that action or not.

2. We should always do things to please Allah سُبْحَانَهُوَتَعَالَى alone, then only will Allah سُبْحَانَهُوَتَعَالَى reward us.

3. Before, after and whilst doing any action we should always check our intention.

4. If shaytaan spoils our intention, then we should ask forgiveness from Allah سُبْحَانَهُوَتَعَالَى and correct our intention.

Story 23

Hadhrat Ali رَضِىَ ٱللّٰهُ عَنْهُ, while fighting with a non-Muslim, managed to drop him and was sitting on top of him ready to kill him with his sword. The non-Muslim spat on Hadhrat Ali's رَضِىَ ٱللّٰهُ عَنْهُ face. This angered Hadhrat Ali رَضِىَ ٱللّٰهُ عَنْهُ. However, he got off the non-Muslim and put his sword away.

As Hadhrat Ali رَضِىَ ٱللّٰهُ عَنْهُ was leaving, the non-Muslim asked, "What is this? After spitting on your face you should have killed me immediately. What stopped you from killing me?" Hadhrat Ali رَضِىَ ٱللّٰهُ عَنْهُ said, "I had the intention of killing you only for the pleasure of Allah سُبْحَانَهُ وَتَعَالَى. When you spat on my face, I became angry. If I had killed you then, it would not have been only for the sake of Allah سُبْحَانَهُ وَتَعَالَى. It would have been because of my anger. Allah سُبْحَانَهُ وَتَعَالَى only accepts those actions which are done only for Him. Therefore I did not kill you."

Hearing this from Hadhrat Ali رَضِىَ ٱللّٰهُ عَنْهُ, the non-Muslim was surprised and Imaan entered his heart. He said, "I happily accept Islam. This Deen is definitely the true Deen."

Story 24

There was a man from the Bani Israeel who used to worship Allah سُبْحَانَهُ وَتَعَالَى all the time. A group of people once came to him and told him that the people of a nearby tribe were worshipping a tree. This news upset him, so he took an axe and went to cut the tree. On the way, shaytaan met him in the disguise of an old man and asked him where he was going. The man told shaytaan that he was going to cut down the tree. Shaytaan said, "The tree has nothing to do with you. Do not leave your Ibaadah for something that does not concern you." "This is also Ibaadah." said the man and continued on his way.

Shaytaan tried to stop him by wrestling with him but the man knocked down shaytaan. Shaytaan begged him to get off him and when the man got off, shaytaan said, "Allah سُبْحَانَهُۥوَتَعَالَى has not made it fardh (compulsory) to cut this tree. If you do not cut this tree, it will not harm you in any way. If cutting the tree was fardh, Allah سُبْحَانَهُۥوَتَعَالَى would have told one of His Prophets to cut it." The man still wanted to cut the tree and shaytaan tried to stop him again. For the second time, the man dropped shaytaan. Shaytaan then said to the man, "You are a poor man. If you do not cut this tree, I will give you three gold coins everyday which you will find under your pillow. With this money you can buy all your things, help your relatives, help the poor and do many other good deeds. Cutting the tree is only one good deed but with the money you can do many good deeds." The man agreed and went back home without cutting the tree.

For two days he found the money under his pillow. However, on the third day he found nothing. He got angry, picked up his axe and set off to cut the tree. On the way, shaytaan met him and asked where he was going. The man replied that he was going to cut the tree. Shaytaan said, "I will not let you cut the tree." This time, when they had a fight, shaytaan knocked down the man. The man was surprised at this and asked shaytaan why he had won the fight this time. Shaytaan said, "The first time when you were going to cut the tree was only for the sake of Allah سُبْحَانَهُوَتَعَالَى. Therefore, Allah سُبْحَانَهُوَتَعَالَى helped you to fight me. This time you were going to cut the tree because you did not get the money. Therefore, I dropped you down."

This time the man was not sincere. He was not doing this action for the pleasure of Allah سُبْحَانَهُوَتَعَالَى.

FRIENDS

قَالَ رَسُوْلُ اللهِ صَلَّى اللهُ عَلَيْهِ وَسَلَّمَ

لَا تُصَاحِبْ اِلَّا مُؤْمِنًا

Do not choose anybody to be your friend except someone
who is a Muslim.

[Abu Dawood]

Lessons Learnt

1. A Muslim should choose his friends carefully.

2. Always check the habits of your friends.

3. If they have any bad habits do not become their friends.

4. Always choose good and pious friends.

5. Always help your friends in need.

'Uqbah bin Abi Mu'eet was one of the leaders in Makkah Mukarramah. It was his habit to invite all the noble people of Makkah to a meal whenever he returned from a journey. He used to meet Rasulullah ﷺ quite often and also invite him for meals.

Once, during one of these meals, he presented the food to Rasulullah ﷺ. Rasulullah ﷺ said, "I cannot eat your food until you say that Allah سُبْحَانَهُ وَتَعَالَى is One and I am His Messenger." 'Uqbah read the kalimah and Rasulullah ﷺ then ate the food. Ubayy bin Khalaf was a close friend of 'Uqbah. When he heard that 'Uqbah had read the kalimah and accepted Islam, he became very angry.

'Uqbah tried to explain to him that Rasulullah ﷺ was a very noble person and if he did not eat the food, 'Uqbah would be disgraced. So, to please Rasulullah ﷺ and to encourage him to eat the food, he read the kalimah. Ubayy did not believe him and said, "If you are true in what you are saying, go and spit in the face of Rasulullah ﷺ." (Na'oozubillah)

'Uqbah listened to his friend and went and spat in the face of Rasulullah ﷺ. Allah سُبْحَانَهُ وَتَعَالَى disgraced both of them in this world and they will be punished severely in the Aakhirah. This is the end result of evil company.

GUARDING THE TONGUE

قَالَ رَسُوْلُ اللهِ صَلَّى اللهُ عَلَيْهِ وَسَلَّمَ

اَمْلِكْ عَلَيْكَ لِسَانَكَ

Guard your tongue.

[Tirmizi]

Lessons Learnt

1. Say good things or remain silent.
2. Think before you speak.
3. Do not say things, which will cause harm to yourself and others such as lying, backbiting, slandering, swearing, etc.
4. Keep your tongue busy in the zikr of Allah سُبْحَانَهُ وَتَعَالَى at all times.
5. Every morning the limbs of the body beg the tongue saying, "If you behave yourself, the rest of us will be saved from trouble but if you misbehave (by saying wrong things, arguing, etc.), the rest of us will be in problems."

Once, the master of Hadhrat Luqmaan عَلَيْهِ ٱلسَّلَام told him to slaughter a sheep and bring to him the best Part of the sheep. Hadhrat Luqmaan عَلَيْهِ ٱلسَّلَام slaughtered a sheep and brought the tongue and the heart. His master told him to slaughter another sheep and bring the worst Parts. Hadhrat Luqmaan عَلَيْهِ ٱلسَّلَام slaughtered another sheep and again brought the tongue and the heart. The master was surprised and asked, "How can these two parts be the best and the worst?" Hadhrat Luqmaan عَلَيْهِ ٱلسَّلَام replied, "If these two parts are used correctly, then they are the best, but if they are used incorrectly, then they are the worst."

Hadith Twenty

JEALOUSY

قَالَ رَسُوۡلُ اللهِ صَلَّى اللهُ عَلَيۡهِ وَسَلَّمَ

اِيَّاكُمۡ وَالۡحَسَدَ

Save yourself from jealousy.

[Abu Dawood]

Lessons Learnt

1. Jealousy means to wish that the wealth, beauty or intelligence that Allah سُبۡحَانَهُۥوَتَعَالَىٰ has given to someone should be snatched away from him and be given to you.

2. Jealousy destroys a person's life and good deeds.

3. It causes grief and pain to the jealous person.

4. Allah سُبۡحَانَهُۥوَتَعَالَىٰ is displeased with a jealous person.

5. Shaytaan was destroyed because he was jealous of Aadam عَلَيۡهِٱلسَّلَامُ.

Haabil and Qaabil were the sons of Hadhrat Aadam عَلَيْهِ ٱلسَّلَامُ. Haabil was told to marry a certain girl and Qaabil was supposed to marry another. The girl who Haabil was supposed to marry was prettier than the one that Qaabil was supposed to marry. Qaabil was jealous and wanted to marry the prettier of the two. This problem was brought to Hadhrat Aadam عَلَيْهِ ٱلسَّلَامُ. In order to sort out the problem, Hadhrat Aadam عَلَيْهِ ٱلسَّلَامُ said, "Both of you should offer something (make qurbaani) to Allah سُبْحَانَهُ وَتَعَالَى. Whoever's offering is accepted will marry the prettier girl."

In those days, a sign of an offering being accepted by Allah سُبْحَانَهُ وَتَعَالَى was that a fire would come down from the sky and eat up the sacrifice. If the fire didn't eat up the offering, it meant that it was not accepted.

Haabil owned sheep and goats so he offered a good, healthy sheep. Qaabil was a farmer so he offered some grains which were not of very good quality. A fire came down from the sky and ate up the offering of Haabil. This made Qaabil angrier and even more jealous. In the end, it was jealousy that made him kill his brother, Haabil.

ANGER

Avoid anger.

[Shu'bul Imaan]

Lessons Learnt

1. It is necessary to control your anger.

2. Shaytaan takes control of a person who does not control his anger.

3. If an angry person is standing he should sit down. If he is sitting he should lie down or move away from the place.

4. When angry, recite Ta'awwuz, drink water or make wudhu.

Story 28

Once, a pious person by the name of Hadhrat Baayazid Bustaami رَحِمَهُ ٱللَّهُ was getting ready for the Eid Salaah. He had a bath, put on clean clothes, applied some itr and set off for the Eidgaah. While passing by a house, someone mistakenly threw some ash from the roof, which landed on him. Instead of getting angry, Hadhrat Baayazid رَحِمَهُ ٱللَّهُ started rubbing the ash on himself and said to himself, "O Baayazid! You were deserving of fire burning you but Allah سُبْحَانَهُ وَتَعَالَى sent only this ash." He went away without even looking up to see who had thrown the ash.

Story 29

Once, shaytaan came to Hadhrat Moosa عَلَيْهِ ٱلسَّلَام and said, "You are the chosen messenger of Allah سُبْحَانَهُ وَتَعَالَى. You speak directly to Allah سُبْحَانَهُ وَتَعَالَى. I wish to repent. I beg you to please speak to Allah سُبْحَانَهُ وَتَعَالَى for me. Hadhrat Moosa عَلَيْهِ ٱلسَّلَام was very happy at this. If shaytaan repented, he would not mislead the people anymore. Everyone would then obey Allah سُبْحَانَهُ وَتَعَالَى. He made wudhu and performed salaah. He then made dua. Allah سُبْحَانَهُ وَتَعَالَى said, "O Moosa, shaytaan is a liar and he wants to bluff you. Tell him if he wishes to make taubah, he should go to the grave of Hadhrat Aadam عَلَيْهِ ٱلسَّلَام and make sajdah there."

Hadhrat Moosa عَلَيْهِ ٱلسَّلَام was again very happy as he thought that this was a very easy thing for shaytaan to do. He gave the message to shaytaan. When shaytaan heard this, he became very angry and said, "How can I make sajdah to that person who is dead when I did not make sajdah to him whilst he was alive."

"Nevertheless, O Moosa عَلَيْهِ ٱلسَّلَام, you have done me a favour. To show thanks for what you have done, I will tell you something. Beware of me at three times:

1. At the time of anger. I am in the heart of a human being and I run in his body like blood.

2. At the battlefield (as well as when learning or teaching Deen or being in the path of Allah سُبْحَانَهُ وَتَعَالَى). At that time I attract the person to his wife, children and belongings so that he may return to them.

3. When a male and female are alone in privacy. I attract them to each other until they both do haraam."

HAVING MERCY ON OTHERS

قَالَ رَسُوْلُ اللهِ صَلَّى اللهُ عَلَيْهِ وَسَلَّمَ

لَا يَرْحَمُ اللهُ مَنْ لَّا يَرْحَمُ النَّاسَ

Allah سُبْحَانَهُوَتَعَالَى does not show mercy to him who does
not show mercy to others.

[Bukhaari]

Lessons Learnt

1. We must be merciful and kind to the creation of Allah
سُبْحَانَهُوَتَعَالَى.

2. We should not ill-treat or harm any creation of Allah
سُبْحَانَهُوَتَعَالَى.

3. Be kind to your servants and workers.

4. Always show kindness to children and to old people.

5. Allah سُبْحَانَهُوَتَعَالَى will show kindness and mercy to a
person who is kind and merciful.

Story 30

In the early days of Islam, the non-Muslims made life very difficult for Rasulullah ﷺ. They mocked him and spat in his face. They threw thorns in his path. They threw the insides of a camel on him. They tried to starve him. They stoned him. His tooth was broken in a battle. His relatives and friends were killed. They even tried to kill him!

When Rasulullah ﷺ took control of Makkah, with 10 000 men, the non-Muslims were afraid. They were weak, helpless and very frightened. He asked them, "How do you want me to treat you?" "With kindness and pity, O noble Brother and Nephew!" they replied.

Tears filled the eyes of Rasulullah ﷺ and he said, "I say to you what Yusuf عَلَيْهِ السَّلَام said to his brother. Have no fear today. Go, you are all free." Rasulullah ﷺ had mercy on all of them.

Story 31

Once, Hadhrat Umar رَضِيَ اللهُ عَنْهُ was walking in the streets when he spotted a tent outside Madinah. When he reached there, he saw a woman with her children. He noticed that the children were crying and that there was a pot placed on the fire. He asked the woman why the children were crying. She replied that they were crying out of hunger. Hadhrat Umar رَضِيَ اللهُ عَنْهُ asked her what was in the pot. She replied that there was only water in the pot to make the children think that something was cooking.

Hadhrat Umar ؓ hurried to Madinah to fetch flour, dates and other things to prepare a meal. He carried the food on his back and he himself prepared the meal and gave it to the lady to feed the children. The lady was pleased with Hadhrat Umar's ؓ kindness and made dua for him.

Grade

Five

LEARNING THE QUR-AAN

قَالَ رَسُوْلُ اللهِ صَلَّى اللهُ عَلَيْهِ وَسَلَّمَ

خَيْرُكُمْ مَنْ تَعَلَّمَ الْقُرْاٰنَ وَعَلَّمَهُ

The best amongst you is he who learns the Qur-aan and
teaches it.

[Bukhaari]

Lessons Learnt

1. The Qur-aan is the greatest gift and blessing of Allah
   سُبْحَانَهُ وَتَعَالَى.

2. Those who are making an effort to learn or teach the Qur-aan are very fortunate as they are the best of all people.

3. We should always try to learn to read the Qur-aan correctly with Tajweed.

4. We should also learn the meaning of the Qur-aan and practice on its teachings.

5. Great rewards have been promised for those who are learning or teaching the Qur-aan.

Hadhrat Zaid bin saabit رَضِىَ اللهُ عَنْهُ was six years old when his father passed away. He was eleven at the time of hijrah. He wanted to take part in the battles of Badr and Uhud but was not allowed because of his young age. He took part in all the battles thereafter.

When the Sahaabah رَضِىَ اللهُ عَنْهُمْ were marching towards Tabuk for battle, the flag of the Banu Maalik tribe was being held by Ammarah رَضِىَ اللهُ عَنْهُ. Rasulullah صَلَّى اللهُ عَلَيْهِ وَسَلَّمَ told him to give it to Hadhrat Zaid رَضِىَ اللهُ عَنْهُ. Ammarah رَضِىَ اللهُ عَنْهُ thought that maybe, someone had complained about him therefore Rasulullah صَلَّى اللهُ عَلَيْهِ وَسَلَّمَ wanted him to give the flag away. He asked, "O Rasulullah صَلَّى اللهُ عَلَيْهِ وَسَلَّمَ, is this because someone complained about me?" Rasulullah صَلَّى اللهُ عَلَيْهِ وَسَلَّمَ replied, "No, because Zaid رَضِىَ اللهُ عَنْهُ knows more Qur-aan than you. This is why he has been chosen."

GOOD CHARACTER

قَالَ رَسُوْلُ اللهِ صَلَّى اللهُ عَلَيْهِ وَسَلَّمَ

Treat others with the best of manners.

[Mishkaat]

Lessons Learnt

1. Treat others in the way you would like to be treated.

2. Do not be harsh and rude. Be kind to all.

3. Allah سُبْحَانَهُوَتَعَالَى loves those who have good manners.

4. The best person is the one who has the best manners.

5. If you lose your wealth you have lost nothing, if you lose your health, you have lost something but if you lose your character, you have lost everything.

There was a man whose servant had left work without taking his pay. The man took the money, bought some seeds and planted them. The crops grew and the man sold them. He took the money and bought more seeds. More crops grew and he made more money. Eventually, with the money he bought a few cattle. As time passed, the cattle multiplied until they formed a large herd.

Sometime later, the servant returned to take his pay which he had forgotten a few years ago. When he asked the man for his pay, the man told him to take the whole herd of cattle. The worker thought that the man was mocking him. The man then explained to him how he had taken his pay and made it grow until it became this large herd of cattle. The worker was very happy and, after thanking the man, took the whole herd away.

Story 34

Hadhrat Waail bin Hujr رَضِىَ اللهُ عَنْهُ was one of the leaders of Hadra-Maut (a city in Yemen). When he accepted Islam, Rasulullah صَلَّى اللهُ عَلَيْهِ وَسَلَّمَ gave him a piece of land in Hadra-Maut and instructed Hadhrat Mu'aawiyyah رَضِىَ اللهُ عَنْهُ to go with him to Yemen and mark off the land for him.

When they left for Yemen, Hadhrat Waail رَضِىَ اللهُ عَنْهُ was sitting on a camel and Hadhrat Mu'aawiyyah رَضِىَ اللهُ عَنْهُ was on foot. As the heat of the desert increased, the hot sand began to burn the feet of Hadhrat Mu'aawiyyah رَضِىَ اللهُ عَنْهُ. He said to Hadhrat Waail رَضِىَ اللهُ عَنْهُ, "It is very hot and the sand is burning my feet. Will you please allow me to sit behind you on the camel so that my feet do not get burnt?" Hadhrat Waail رَضِىَ اللّٰهُ عَنْهُ replied, "You are not fit to sit behind kings on the same animal. However, you may walk in the shadow of my camel." In this way Hadhrat Mu'aawiyyah رَضِىَ اللّٰهُ عَنْهُ walked the whole way, from Madinah Munawwarah to Yemen, . When they reached Yemen, Hadhrat Mu'aawiyyah رَضِىَ اللّٰهُ عَنْهُ marked off the land for Hadhrat Waail رَضِىَ اللّٰهُ عَنْهُ and thereafter returned to Madinah Munawwarah.

After many years, Allah سُبْحَانَهُ وَتَعَالَى made Hadhrat Mu'aawiyyah رَضِىَ اللّٰهُ عَنْهُ the Khaleefah (Muslim ruler). Hadhrat Waail رَضِىَ اللّٰهُ عَنْهُ left Yemen and came to Damascus to meet him. When Hadhrat Mu'aawiyyah رَضِىَ اللّٰهُ عَنْهُ came to know of this, he went outside the city to welcome Hadhrat Waail رَضِىَ اللّٰهُ عَنْهُ. He honoured him and treated him nicely and not once did he ever remind him about the treatment he received from him many years ago.

MODESTY

قَالَ رَسُوْلُ اللهِ صَلَّى اللهُ عَلَيْهِ وَسَلَّمَ

اَلْحَيَاءُ شُعْبَةٌ مِّنَ الْاِيْمَانِ

Modesty is part of Imaan.

[Bukhaari]

Lessons Learnt

1. A person who has true Imaan will always be decent and not rude.

2. Modesty and shame should be shown in everything.

3. A persons' speech, dressing and manners should always be respectful.

4. Imaan and modesty are joined to each other. If a persons' modesty is lost, he may also lose his Imaan.

5. Boys and girls lose their shame when they mix freely with each other.

6. Dressing correctly plays an important role in modesty. We should always dress modestly and protect our shame.

Hadhrat Aaisha رَضِيَ ٱللّٰهُ عَنْهَا had great knowledge of Deen. Once, a blind man came to her to ask her some matter of Deen. When this blind person came, she immediately covered her face. The man sensed this and asked, "I am blind, why are you making purdah from me?" Hadhrat Aaisha رَضِيَ ٱللّٰهُ عَنْهَا said, "You are blind but I am not blind. You cannot see me but I can see you."

GRATITUDE (TO SHOW THANKS)

قَالَ رَسُوْلُ اللهِ صَلَّى اللهُ عَلَيْهِ وَسَلَّمَ

مَنْ لَّمْ يَشْكُرِ النَّاسَ لَمْ يَشْكُرِ اللهَ

He who does not thank people cannot thank Allah.

[Tirmizi]

Lessons Learnt

1. We should always thank those who help us.

2. We may give them a gift or write a note to show our thanks.

3. We should always be thankful to Allah سُبْحَانَهُ وَتَعَالَى who provides all our needs.

4. By being grateful and thankful, Allah سُبْحَانَهُ وَتَعَالَى will increase his favours upon us.

5. We should thank others by saying '*JazakaAllah*'.

6. Always be grateful to your parents because you enjoyed the most favours from them.

Hadhrat Luqmaan عَلَيْهِ ٱلسَّلَامُ was the slave of a rich man. The good character of Hadhrat Luqmaan عَلَيْهِ ٱلسَّلَامُ had such an effect on his master that his master used to treat him like a very close friend. It was the habit of the master that whenever he had anything special to eat, he would let Hadhrat Luqmaan عَلَيْهِ ٱلسَّلَامُ eat first and he would eat the leftovers. Hadhrat Luqmaan عَلَيْهِ ٱلسَّلَامُ thought of the love his master had for him and would eat a little and then send the rest of the food to his master. One day, during the melon season, the master received a melon from somewhere. At that time Hadhrat Luqmaan عَلَيْهِ ٱلسَّلَامُ was not there. The master sent someone to call him. When Hadhrat Luqmaan عَلَيْهِ ٱلسَّلَامُ came, the master cut the melon into slices and started feeding them to him, slice after slice. Hadhrat Luqmaan عَلَيْهِ ٱلسَّلَامُ ate the slices as though he was really enjoying them and all the time thanked his master.

When there was one slice left, the master said, "Let me eat this slice and see how sweet this melon is." Saying this, he put a piece into his mouth. The melon was so bitter that it caused him to faint. When he got up, he asked Hadhrat Luqmaan عَلَيْهِ ٱلسَّلَامُ, "How could you eat all those slices with such enjoyment when one piece of it made me faint?"

Hadhrat Luqmaan عَلَيْهِ ٱلسَّلَامُ replied, "O Master! I have received hundreds of gifts from you. It would be very ungrateful of me to complain of one bitter melon after enjoying hundreds of favours from you."

TAQWA (FEAR OF ALLAH)

قَالَ رَسُوْلُ اللهِ صَلَّى اللهُ عَلَيْهِ وَسَلَّمَ

اِتَّقِ اللهَ حَيْثُ مَا كُنْتَ

Fear Allah سُبْحَانَهُ وَتَعَالَى wherever you are.

[Shu'bul Imaan]

Lessons Learnt

1. Taqwa means to fear Allah سُبْحَانَهُ وَتَعَالَى in every place or condition. Allah سُبْحَانَهُ وَتَعَالَى is observing us every moment of our lives.

2. Taqwa is to fulfil every command of Allah سُبْحَانَهُ وَتَعَالَى and to protect oneself from his disobedience by not doing any sin.

3. Allah سُبْحَانَهُ وَتَعَالَى loves those who have the quality of Taqwa.

4. A person who has Taqwa will be very close to Rasulullah صَلَّى اللهُ عَلَيْهِ وَسَلَّمَ on the Day of Qiyaamah.

Story 37

Hadhrat Umar رَضِىَاللهُعَنْهُ was the leader of the Muslims. One night he was walking in the streets of Madinah. As he passed one of the houses, he heard two people talking. A woman was saying to her daughter, "Let us mix some water with the milk. We can make more money. We are poor and we need the money. Nobody will know what we did."

"No," said the daughter. "It is wrong to mix water with the milk and then to sell it. It is against the order of Hadhrat Umar رَضِىَاللهُعَنْهُ. It is dishonest."

The mother said, "Hadhrat Umar رَضِىَاللهُعَنْهُ is not here. He will not know what we are doing." "We must obey Hadhrat Umar رَضِىَاللهُعَنْهُ, even if he is not here," said the daughter. "Besides, he may not know, but how can we hide from Allah سُبْحَانَهُوَتَعَالَى? He sees everything and He knows everything."

Hadhrat Umar رَضِىَاللهُعَنْهُ walked off silently. He was very pleased with the girl.

Story 38

Once, while Hadhrat Umar رَضِىَاللهُعَنْهُ was travelling, he saw a shepherd grazing a flock of sheep. He asked for some milk since the Arabs used to give travellers milk to drink for free. The shepherd apologised and said, "I am not the owner of these sheep. I am only a shepherd. I do not have the owner's permission to give you the milk."

Hadhrat Umar رَضِيَ ٱللَّهُ عَنْهُ decided to test him. He said to the shepherd, "Let me tell you something which will be good for both of us. You sell me a goat. I will enjoy its milk. You can take the money for yourself. As for the owner, tell him that a wolf ate up the sheep. He will believe you because there are many wolves in this area." After hearing this, the shepherd immediately started saying,

"Then where is Allah سُبْحَانَهُ وَتَعَالَى? Then where is Allah سُبْحَانَهُ وَتَعَالَى?"

(What the shepherd meant was that have you forgotten that Allah سُبْحَانَهُ وَتَعَالَى is watching? Maybe I can lie to the owner and take away the money, but can I hide from Allah سُبْحَانَهُ وَتَعَالَى?).

Hadhrat Umar رَضِيَ ٱللَّهُ عَنْهُ was very pleased with his reply. He later bought the shepherd (who was a slave) and freed him. He also gave him many sheep as a gift.

DUROOD SHAREEF

قَالَ رَسُوْلُ اللهِ صَلَّى اللهُ عَلَيْهِ وَسَلَّمَ

مَنْ صَلَّى عَلَيَّ وَاحِدَةً صَلَّى اللهُ عَلَيْهِ عَشْرًا

One who sends one durood upon me, Allah سُبْحَانَهُ وَتَعَالَى will bless him ten times.

[Muslim]

Lessons Learnt

1. Our Nabi صَلَّى اللهُ عَلَيْهِ وَسَلَّمَ made great sacrifices for us. He went through many difficulties for us.

2. We should send lots and lots of Durood and Salaam on him because of all his favours on us.

3. By sending Durood upon Nabi صَلَّى اللهُ عَلَيْهِ وَسَلَّمَ, the love of Nabi صَلَّى اللهُ عَلَيْهِ وَسَلَّمَ will enter our hearts.

4. A person who does not send Durood after hearing the name of our Nabi صَلَّى اللهُ عَلَيْهِ وَسَلَّمَ is a miser or a stingy person.

5. We should at least send 100 Durood upon our Nabi صَلَّى اللهُ عَلَيْهِ وَسَلَّمَ daily.

6. We should increase our recitation of durood on Fridays.

Story 39

Allah سُبْحَانَهُوَتَعَالَى once told Hadhrat Moosa عَلَيْهِٱلسَّلَامُ, "O Moosa عَلَيْهِٱلسَّلَامُ, if there were no people on earth to make My Zikr, I would neither send down a single drop of rain nor would I allow a single seed to grow. O Moosa عَلَيْهِٱلسَّلَامُ, do you wish to become very close to me?" Hadhrat Moosa عَلَيْهِٱلسَّلَامُ said, "Yes indeed O Allah سُبْحَانَهُوَتَعَالَى." Allah سُبْحَانَهُوَتَعَالَى said, "Read lots of Durood on Nabi Muhammad صَلَّىٱللَّهُعَلَيْهِوَسَلَّمَ."

Story 40

Ubaidullah bin Umar رَضِىَٱللَّهُعَنْهُ says, "I once had a close friend who was a writer. After he died, I saw him in a dream and asked him how Allah سُبْحَانَهُوَتَعَالَى had treated him. He said that Allah سُبْحَانَهُوَتَعَالَى had forgiven him. I asked him what action of his was liked by Allah سُبْحَانَهُوَتَعَالَى for which Allah سُبْحَانَهُوَتَعَالَى had forgiven him. He replied that whenever he used to write the name of Rasulullah صَلَّىٱللَّهُعَلَيْهِوَسَلَّمَ, he used to always add صَلَّىٱللَّهُعَلَيْهِوَسَلَّمَ. For this Allah سُبْحَانَهُوَتَعَالَى gave him what no eye has seen, no ear has heard of and no heart has imagined."

Grade Six

DUA

قَالَ رَسُوْلُ اللهِ صَلَّى اللهُ عَلَيْهِ وَسَلَّمَ

اَلدُّعَاءُ مُخُّ الْعِبَادَةِ

Dua is the essence (flavour) of Ibaadah.

[Tirmizi]

Lessons Learnt

1. Dua means to beg Allah سُبْحَانَهُوَتَعَالَى for our needs.

2. Dua must be made with humbleness and sincerity.

3. Dua can be made in any language.

4. Dua is a weapon for a believer to solve his problems.

5. For our duas to be accepted we should make sure that our food and earnings are always Halaal.

6. We should ask Allah سُبْحَانَهُوَتَعَالَى for all our needs of this world as well as the next.

Hadhrat Rabi'ah Basriah رَحِمَهَا اللّٰه was a lady who was very pious. Once, she was going to Makkah Mukarramah to perform Haj. She had an old donkey to carry her luggage. On the way the donkey died. Her friends offered to carry her goods but she refused. The caravan moved on and Rabi'ah رَحِمَهَا اللّٰه was left alone.

She then made dua to Allah سُبْحَانَهُ وَتَعَالَى, "O Master of the worlds! I am alone, weak and poor. You have invited me to Your house and now my donkey has died, leaving me all alone. Please help me." Allah سُبْحَانَهُ وَتَعَالَى answered his dua.

At once the donkey became alive. She put her goods on it and continued her journey.

GIFTS

قَالَ رَسُوْلُ اللهِ صَلَّى اللهُ عَلَيْهِ وَسَلَّمَ

تَهَادَوْا تَحَآبُّوْا

Give gifts to each other you will love each other.

[Al-Adabul Mufrad]

Lessons Learnt

1. Muslims should always love one another.

2. By giving gifts to another Muslim it shows our love for him.

3. Giving of gifts removes hatred from the heart.

4. If we give someone a gift we should never ask him to return it.

5. We should make a habit of giving gifts to one another.

6. We should not feel shy to give simple things as gifts.

During interval at school, all the boys would sit in a classroom and eat the lunch their mother had packed for them. Each day as Bilal ate his lunch, he would notice Yusuf sitting alone. Yusuf did not bring lunch. While all the other boys were eating, Yusuf would sit quietly or put his head on the desk.

Bilal began to wonder why Yusuf never brought lunch to school. He noticed that Yusuf was very thin, and that He did not have as much energy as the other boys. His clothes and shoes also looked very old. He realised that Yusuf's family probably did not have enough money for Yusuf to bring lunch to school.

Bilal had been taught that Allah loves and rewards kindness. One day He sat next to Yusuf and asked, "Would you please help me eat my lunch?" Yusuf was surprised. He was also very hungry, so he agreed. That was the first day that Bilal and Yusuf ate lunch together. Yusuf remembered to thank Bilal by saying "Jazakallah", which means, "May Allah reward you."

Thereafter, Bilal would always share lunch with Yusuf. They soon became very close friends. Yusuf explained to Bilal why he didn't bring lunch everyday. He said, "My parents do not have much money. That is why we can only eat in the morning and evening. We make dua to Allah everyday to make it easy for us. Insha Allah our duas will soon be answered."

Bilal liked sharing his lunch with Yusuf. Yusuf, however, felt sad that he could not give Bilal anything in return. He said, "Bilal, everyday you share your lunch with me but I can't share anything with you. I wish there was something I could do for you."

Bilal thought about it for a moment. Then he smiled and said, "My mother always says that the best gift that you can give a person is to make dua for them. If you really want to do something for me, then make dua for me."

Yusuf agreed that it was a good idea. From then onwards he began to make dua for Bilal everyday. Eventually, Yusuf's parents could afford to give his lunch everyday. He and Bilal still liked to share though. Now they had two lunches to share. Through sharing, Yusuf and Bilal remained close friends. Yusuf has never forgotten how wonderful Bilal was to him. He still continues to make dua for his special friend.

CHEATING

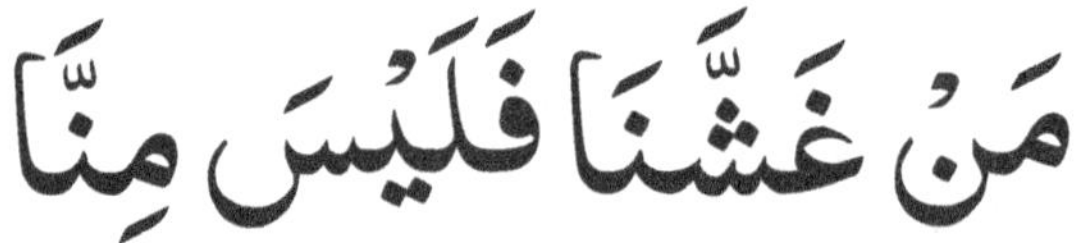

قَالَ رَسُوْلُ اللهِ صَلَّى اللهُ عَلَيْهِ وَسَلَّمَ

مَنْ غَشَّنَا فَلَيْسَ مِنَّا

He who cheats us is not one of us.

[Kanzul Ummaal]

Lessons Learnt

1. Cheating and deceiving are evil habits.

2. They are major sins.

3. Cheating includes lying, tricking, bluffing and misleading others.

4. The cure for deception is to be truthful at all times.

5. Rasulullah ﷺ did not want to have anything to do with a person who cheats and deceives.

6. No one likes to be friends with someone who cheats and tricks others.

Rasulullah ﷺ once passed by a person who was selling a heap of grain. Rasulullah ﷺ put his mubaarak hand inside the heap and took out some grains which were wet. Rasulullah ﷺ asked him how the grains got wet. The man said that it got wet in the rain so he put the dry grain on top to hide it. Rasulullah ﷺ told him to leave the wet grains on top so that the people will be able to see them otherwise he will be cheating them. Thereafter Rasulullah ﷺ said, "He who cheats us is not one of us."

NOTE: Wet grain increases the weight and is of a lower quality.

OBSCENE (RUDE) TALK

لَمْ يَكُنْ رَسُوْلُ اللهِ صَلَّى اللهُ عَلَيْهِ وَسَلَّمَ
فَاحِشًا وَّلَا مُتَفَحِّشًا

Nabi ﷺ was not a rude person nor did he behave rudely.

[Bukhaari]

Lessons Learnt

1. A Muslim is never rude in his behaviour or in his speech.

2. If anyone is rude to you, never behave rudely to him, rather treat him with kindness.

3. We should never swear anyone or behave in a shameless manner.

4. Always speak kindly and decently to all people even the beggars on the road.

Hadhrat Anas رَضِىَ اللّٰهُ عَنْهُ says, "I was once walking with Rasulullah صَلَّى اللّٰهُ عَلَيْهِ وَسَلَّم. He was wearing a shawl made of rough material. A villager came up to Rasulullah صَلَّى اللّٰهُ عَلَيْهِ وَسَلَّم, grabbed the shawl and pulled Rasulullah صَلَّى اللّٰهُ عَلَيْهِ وَسَلَّم towards him. He pulled Rasulullah صَلَّى اللّٰهُ عَلَيْهِ وَسَلَّم so hard that the shawl actually left a mark on his blessed shoulder. The villager then said (very rudely and disrespectfully), 'O Muhammad! Give me some of the wealth that is by you which belongs to Allah سُبْحَانَهُ وَتَعَالَى.' (Look at the tolerance and beautiful character of Rasulullah صَلَّى اللّٰهُ عَلَيْهِ وَسَلَّم). Rasulullah صَلَّى اللّٰهُ عَلَيْهِ وَسَلَّم smiled and told one of the Sahaabah to give this villager some wealth."

Some of the people who were standing around Rasulullah صَلَّى اللّٰهُ عَلَيْهِ وَسَلَّم got very angry. They wanted to hit the villager but Nabi صَلَّى اللّٰهُ عَلَيْهِ وَسَلَّم stopped them and commanded not to behave badly towards him.

HUMILITY

قَالَ رَسُوْلُ اللهِ صَلَّى اللهُ عَلَيْهِ وَسَلَّمَ

مَنْ تَوَاضَعَ لِلّٰهِ رَفَعَهُ اللهُ

He who humbles himself for the sake of Allah سُبْحَانَهُ وَتَعَالَى,
Allah سُبْحَانَهُ وَتَعَالَى will elevate him in rank.

[Shu'bul Imaan]

Lessons Learnt

1. Being humble means to believe that others are better than you. This will help you in serving others.

2. If you have a high position or lots of wealth then you should be more careful because these qualities can create pride in your heart.

3. We should always feel that we are lower than all Allah's سُبْحَانَهُ وَتَعَالَى creation.

4. The more we will humble ourselves, the more Allah Ta'ala will grant us honour and respect.

Story 45

Hadhrat Salmaan Farsi رَضِيَ اللهُ عَنْهُ was the governor of Madinah Munawwarah. Once, he was walking through the market when someone thought that he was a slave. That person told him to pick up his load. Hadhrat Salmaan رَضِيَ اللهُ عَنْهُ happily picked up the load and carried it for the man. When the people saw this, many requested that he give the load to them but he refused.

After some time the person realised who was carrying his load. He became worried and begged Hadhrat Salmaan رَضِيَ اللهُ عَنْهُ to forgive him. Hadhrat Salmaan رَضِيَ اللهُ عَنْهُ told him not to worry. The man felt ashamed of what he had done and took an oath never to give his load to anybody to carry.

Story 46

Hadhrat Umar's رَضِيَ اللهُ عَنْهُ journey to Baitul Muqaddas is well known. He and his slave were travelling on one camel. For a certain distance, Hadhrat Umar رَضِيَ اللهُ عَنْهُ would ride and his slave would lead it, and for the same distance the slave would ride and Hadhrat Umar رَضِيَ اللهُ عَنْهُ would lead it.

At one stage it was Hadhrat Umar's رَضِيَ اللهُ عَنْهُ turn to lead the camel when they had to pass through water. He took off his shoes and, holding them under his arms, entered the water and crossed. When they neared Baitul Muqaddas, it was once again the turn of Hadhrat Umar رَضِيَ اللهُ عَنْهُ to lead the camel. Hadhrat Abu Ubaidah رَضِيَ اللهُ عَنْهُ, who was waiting for Hadhrat Umar رَضِيَ اللهُ عَنْهُ, saw this and said, "O Ameerul Mumineen, the people of the city will come to welcome you. It is not proper that you lead the camel while the slave rides on it. You should be riding the camel." Hadhrat Umar رَضِيَ اللهُ عَنْهُ replied, "Allah سُبْحَانَهُ وَتَعَالَى had honoured us through Islam. Your suggestion will make me to be unjust to my slave. Should I be unjust only to impress people?"

NEIGHBOURS

قَالَ رَسُوْلُ اللهِ صَلَّى اللهُ عَلَيْهِ وَسَلَّمَ

خَيْرُ الْجِيْرَانِ عِنْدَ اللهِ خَيْرُهُمْ لِجَارِهِ

The best neighbour in the sight of Allah سُبْحَانَهُوَتَعَالَى is he who is good to his neighbour.

[Mustadrak Haakim]

Lessons Learnt

1. We should always be kind to our neighbours. Never harm them in any way.

2. We should always be the first to help them if they are in any problem.

3. We should share our food with them. If they are poor we should help them.

4. We should not do anything which will hurt them like disturbing them when they are asleep or burning a fire near their home.

5. If they hurt us we should be patient and forgive them.

Story 47

One of the neighbours of Hadhrat Bayaazid Bustami رحمة الله was a fire-worshipper. This neighbour once went on a journey, leaving behind his wife and his small child. At night the child would become restless and cry because of the darkness. (They didn't have a lamp). When Hadhrat Bayaazid رحمة الله came to know of this, he would light his lamp and leave it at the neighbour's house at night. Because of the light, the child would calm down and sleep soundly. When the fire-worshipper returned, his wife told him of the kindness of Hadhrat Bayaazid رحمة الله. This had such an effect on the fire-worshipper that he immediately went next door and accepted Islam at the hands of Hadhrat Bayaazid رحمة الله.

Story 48

One of the neighbours of Imaam Abu Haneefah رحمة الله was a shoemaker. During the day he would be busy making and fixing shoes and at night he would get drunk and sing till late, causing a disturbance. Every night, whilst performing Salaah, Imaam Abu Haneefah رحمة الله would hear him making noise.

One night, Imaam Abu Haneefah رحمة الله did not hear him making noise. He found out that the police had arrested the shoemaker. The next morning, immediately after Salaah, Imaam Saahib رحمة الله went to the house of the governor of the city. The governor welcomed him and asked if he needed anything. Imaam Saahib رحمة الله said, "One of my neighbours has been arrested. Can you please free him?" The governor ordered that Imaam Saahib's

رَحِمَهُ ٱللَّه neighbour be set free as well as all the other prisoners who were arrested on that day.

As Imaam Saahib رَحِمَهُ ٱللَّه was returning from the governor's house, his neighbour, who was now freed, ran up to him and said, "You have been so kind to me. May Allah سُبْحَانَهُ وَتَعَالَى grant you the greatest reward for protecting your neighbour"

The shoemaker repented (made taubah) from drinking alcohol. He then began to attend the gatherings of Imaam Saahib رَحِمَهُ ٱللَّه until he became one of the famous Aalim of the time.

Grade Seven

WEALTH

قَالَ رَسُوْلُ اللهِ صَلَّى اللهُ عَلَيْهِ وَسَلَّمَ

اِنَّ لِكُلِّ اُمَّةٍ فِتْنَةً وَ فِتْنَةُ اُمَّتِيْ اَلْمَالُ

Every Ummah (group of people) had a test. The test of my
Ummah is wealth.

[Tirmizi]

Lessons Learnt

1. The test of wealth means that neither should we be greedy for wealth nor should we misuse the wealth Allah سُبْحَانَهُوَتَعَالَى has provided us with.

2. Having wealth or money is not harmful as long as we use it correctly.

3. We should not wish for more than what Allah سُبْحَانَهُوَتَعَالَى has fixed for us.

4. We should always thank Allah سُبْحَانَهُوَتَعَالَى for what He has provided us and trust in Him alone to help us.

5. We should always spend in the path of Allah سُبْحَانَهُوَتَعَالَى by helping the poor and needy.

A poor man by the name of Th'alabah ibn Haatib came to Rasulullah ﷺ and asked Rasulullah ﷺ to make dua that he becomes wealthy. Rasulullah ﷺ said, "Don't you like my way (of simplicity and poverty)? I take an oath in that Being who controls my life that if I wished, the mountains of Madinah would turn into gold and follow me wherever I go. However, I do not like such riches." Th'alabah went away.

After some time he came back and made the same request and also promised that if he became wealthy, he would use his money correctly. Rasulullah ﷺ made dua that he becomes wealthy. The result of this dua was that the few goats which he had began to increase. They increased so much that he had to move just outside Madinah. Thus he used to perform only Zuhr and Asr with Rasulullah ﷺ whilst the rest of the Salaahs he performed at home. Thereafter his goats increased even more and he had to move right out of Madinah. Then he used to come for Jumu'ah Salaah only. Eventually he had to move even further out of Madinah and stopped coming for even the Jumu'ah Salaah.

Meanwhile the aayaat of Zakaat were revealed. Rasulullah ﷺ wrote out in detail the Zakaat that should be taken from those who own animals. Rasulullah ﷺ then gave the paper to two Sahaabah and told them to collect the Zakaat from the people. He also specifically instructed them to go to Th'alabah and another person from the Banu Sulaim tribe.

When these two people reached Th'alabah and showed him the paper of Rasulullah ﷺ, he said, "This is Kharaaj (tax taken from non-Muslims). Carry on with your work. On your way back, stop by me again."

The two of them then went to the person from the Banu Sulaim tribe. When he saw how much Zakaat he had to give from his animals, he chose the best animals and happily gave it to them. They said, "You have brought the best animals whereas we have been instructed to take the average animal, not the highest quality nor the lowest quality. Thus we cannot take these animals." However this person insisted that they take the best animal. They then went and collected Zakaat from the other people.

On their return, they again stopped by Th'alabah. He asked them to show him the paper on which the details of the Zakaat were written. After looking at it again, he said, "This is a tax which is not to be taken from Muslims. Carry on back to Madinah. I will think about it for a while before I make a decision."

When they returned to Madinah, they told Rasulullah ﷺ what had happened. Rasulullah ﷺ was pleased with the man from the Banu Sulaim tribe and made dua that Allah ﷻ give him lots of Barakah in his life. When Rasulullah ﷺ heard about Th'alabah, he said thrice, "Woe (destruction) be on Th'alabah!" Aayaat of the Qur-aan were then revealed about Th'alabah. A friend of Th'alabah who was present immediately went to Th'alabah, scolded him and told him what had happened.

Th'alabah rushed to Madinah with his Zakaat and begged Rasulullah ﷺ to accept it. Rasulullah ﷺ said, "I have been commanded by Allah سُبْحَانَهُوَتَعَالَى not to accept your Zakaat. When I had sent my instruction to you, you did not obey. Now your Zakaat cannot be accepted."

Shortly thereafter Rasulullah ﷺ passed away. When Hadhrat Abu Bakr رَضِىَاللهُعَنْهُ was the Khaleefah, Th'alabah brought his Zakaat to him. Hadhrat Abu Bakr رَضِىَاللهُعَنْهُ said, "How can I accept what Rasulullah ﷺ did not accept?" When Hadhrat Umar رَضِىَاللهُعَنْهُ became the Khaleefah, Th'alabah again brought his Zakaat. Hadhrat Umar رَضِىَاللهُعَنْهُ said, "How can I accept what Rasulullah ﷺ and Hadhrat Abu Bakr رَضِىَاللهُعَنْهُ did not accept?" When Hadhrat Usmaan رَضِىَاللهُعَنْهُ became the Khaleefah, Th'alabah once again brought his Zakaat. Hadhrat Usmaan رَضِىَاللهُعَنْهُ said, "How can I accept that which was not accepted by Rasulullah ﷺ, Hadhrat Abu Bakr رَضِىَاللهُعَنْهُ and Hadhrat Umar رَضِىَاللهُعَنْهُ?" Th'alabah died during the rule of Hadhrat Usmaan رَضِىَاللهُعَنْهُ.

[Tafseer-e-Usmaani Page 893]

DOUBTFUL THINGS

قَالَ رَسُوْلُ اللهِ صَلَّى اللهُ عَلَيْهِ وَسَلَّمَ

دَعْ مَا يُرِيْبُكَ إِلَى مَا لَا يُرِيْبُكَ

Leave out those things which are doubtful for those things that are not doubtful.

[Tirmizi]

Lessons Learnt

1. If a person is in doubt about whether something is halaal or not, he should stay away from it.

2. Use only things that are not doubtful.

3. Stay away from doubtful foods. Do not eat such food which you are not sure of.

4. A person who avoids doubtful things looks after his Imaan and his honour.

5. A person who uses doubtful things might do something haraam.

6. Remember, **"When in doubt leave it out"** or **"first find out"**.

Hadhrat Abu Bakr رَضِیَ اللّٰہُ عَنْہُ had a slave who used to give him some of his daily wages. Once, the slave brought some food from which Hadhrat Abu Bakr رَضِیَ اللّٰہُ عَنْہُ took a bite. The slave said, "You always first ask me where I get the food from, but today you did not ask." Hadhrat Abu Bakr رَضِیَ اللّٰہُ عَنْہُ replied, "I was so hungry that I forgot. Tell me now, how did you get this food?" The slave said, "Before I became a Muslim, I used to do fortune-telling (which is haraam). I did some fortune-telling for some people who promised to pay me later. I saw those people today celebrating a wedding and they gave me this food."

Abu Bakr رَضِیَ اللّٰہُ عَنْہُ said, "Ah! This will kill me." He then tried to vomit the food which he had swallowed but could not do so as his stomach had been quite empty. Somebody suggested that he drink water to his fill and then try to vomit. He kept on drinking water and vomiting until the morsel came out. Somebody said, "May Allah سُبْحَانَہُ وَتَعَالٰی have mercy on you! You put yourself through such difficulty for a single bite."

Hadhrat Abu Bakr رَضِیَ اللّٰہُ عَنْہُ said, "I would have taken it out even if I had to lose my life. I have heard Rasulullah صَلَّی اللّٰہُ عَلَیْہِ وَسَلَّم saying, 'The flesh that is fed by haraam food will go into the fire of Jahannam.' I therefore quickly tried to vomit that bite before any part of my body should receive nourishment from it."

The pious people would not eat anything until they were perfectly sure that it was halaal. If there was the slightest doubt, they would not eat it and if by mistake they ate it, they would immediately vomit it out.

Story 51

Hadhrat Umar رَضِيَ ٱللَّهُ عَنْهُ once received some musk (expensive perfume) from Bahrain. He said, "I want someone to weigh it so that it may be equally distributed among the Muslims." His wife said, "I shall weigh it." Hadhrat Umar رَضِيَ ٱللَّهُ عَنْهُ kept quiet. A little later he again asked for someone to weigh the musk and again his wife volunteered to do so. Again, Hadhrat Umar رَضِيَ ٱللَّهُ عَنْهُ kept quiet. When she offered for the third time, Hadhrat Umar رَضِيَ ٱللَّهُ عَنْهُ said, "I do not like you touching the musk while weighing it and rubbing it on yourself afterwards as this would amount to something more than my share."

Any other person weighing the musk would have had the same advantage but Hadhrat Umar رَضِيَ ٱللَّهُ عَنْهُ did not like this for any member of his own family. Look at this cautiousness to avoid even the slightest bit of doubt.

INTOXICANTS (THINGS THAT MAKE A PERSON DRUNK)

All intoxicants are haraam (unlawful).

[Bukhaari]

Lessons Learnt

1. Intoxicants are those things that cause a person to lose his mind and intelligence.

2. Intoxicants may also be in the form of drugs or in a liquid form such as wine and other types of alcohol.

3. **Intoxicants can cause a person to commit all types of evil actions.**

4. Muslims must never touch alcohol or any kind of drugs.

Once, a king caught a man and said, "If you do not kill this child, or commit sin with this woman or drink wine, I will kill you." The man thought to himself that the least harmful of the three was to drink the wine. In a drunken state, he killed the child and committed sin with that woman.

From this story we learn that alcohol is the root of all sins. It causes a person to do many other sins.

BEING ALONE WITH A FEMALE

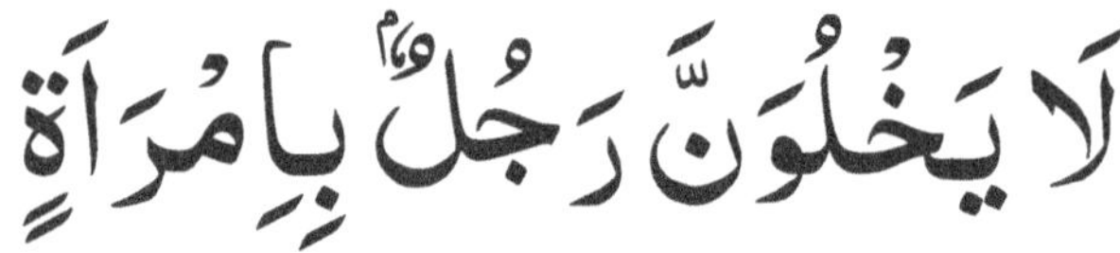

No male should be alone with a strange female.

[Bukhaari]

Lessons Learnt

1. If a strange male and female are alone then the third person is Shaytaan. Strange means that they are not blood relatives eg. (Father and daughter, Mother and son or brother and sister).

2. Shaytaan will try his best to make them do haraam as he becomes the messenger between the two of them.

3. A person should be careful not to go to such places where he will be alone with a female.

4. **A strange male and female may only remain alone in privacy once they are married.**

There was a very famous pious man in the Bani Israeel. He used to stay alone in his monastery (place of worship) and busy himself in the worship of Allah سُبْحَانَهُوَتَعَالَى. There were three brothers and their sister also staying in that area. The three brothers were called to go out in jihaad. They were worried about the safety of their sister. After making mashwara (i.e. after holding a meeting) they decided to leave her by the pious man. They trusted him because of his piety.

When they told him of their intention of leaving their sister with him he refused. After much insistence and begging, he finally agreed to look after their sister. He told them to leave her in a small house which was next to his monastery. They left her there and went out in jihaad.

In the beginning, the pious man used to take some food and leave it outside the door of the house. He would then go back to his room and from there tell her that her food was by the door. Slowly shaytaan began to whisper to him, "The poor girl is alone. She has no family with her and she doesn't know anybody else. At least speak to her a little so that she won't feel so lonely." Thus he began to speak to her a little but from outside the house (He was outside while she was inside). As time went, they began talking for longer and longer until a time came when they began to speak to one another for the whole day.

Then shaytaan again began to whisper to him, "It is rude to speak to someone while you are outside and the other person is inside. Show good manners by going inside the house and speak to her." Thus he began to go inside the house to speak to her. Within a very short time, shaytaan got them involved in sin. After some time she gave birth to a son. Shaytaan began to frighten the pious man about what will happen when her brothers return. In this fear he killed their sister and her child, dug a hole in which he placed their bodies and placed a big rock over it.

When the brothers returned to fetch their sister, the monk told them that she got very sick and died. He then took them to a place and said that this was where he buried her. (That was not the real place where her body was) The brothers were very sad over the death of their sister. That night, shaytaan came in the dream of all the brothers and told them that the monk lied to them. Actually he fathered a child from her then killed her and her child. He then showed them the place where their bodies were buried.

In the morning the brothers realised that they all had the same dream. They went to the place which they were shown in the dream. They moved the rock, dug up the hole and found the bodies of their sister and her child. They then came to the pious man and told him what they had seen in their dream. The pious man owned up that he had done these evil things.

The brothers then took the pious man to the king who decided that he should be killed. Just before he could be killed, shaytaan came up to the man and said, "It was I who encouraged the brothers to leave their sister with you, it was I who made you to speak to her, it was I who made you to go inside the house, it was I who involved you in sin and it was I who told the brothers the truth. I put you in all these problems. Now if you believe in me and disbelieve in Allah سُبْحَانَهُ وَتَعَالَى, I will get you out of all these problems." At that moment he disbelieved in Allah سُبْحَانَهُ وَتَعَالَى and he was killed as a kaafir. May Allah سُبْحَانَهُ وَتَعَالَى save us from such an evil death. *Aameen.*

CRYING OVER ONE'S SINS

قَالَ رَسُوْلُ اللهِ صَلَّى اللهُ عَلَيْهِ وَسَلَّمَ

وَابْكِ عَلٰى خَطِيْئَتِكَ

Cry over your sins.

[Tirmizi]

Lessons Learnt

1. Crying over our sins means that we should regret over the sins we commit.

2. Sins destroy a person in this world and the hereafter.

3. Stay away from all sins.

4. Ask forgiveness from Allah سُبْحَانَهُوَتَعَالَى at all times, especially, after doing an evil action.

5. Seek forgiveness at least a hundred times daily. We should seek forgiveness by saying, *"Astaghfirullah"*.

6. If you harmed or hurt someone, then ask him for forgiveness.

Hadhrat Maalik bin Dinaar رحمة الله عليه was a very pious man. He was a great sinner before he became pious. He explains how he changed his life.

He says, "When I was young, I was a policeman who was very fond of alcohol. I had a daughter whom I loved very much. When she learnt how to talk and walk, I loved her even more. Whenever she used to see me holding a glass of alcohol, she would take it and spill it on my clothes. I never shouted at her because I loved her very much. When she was two years old, she passed away and I was extremely sad.

One night I was drunk and went to sleep without reading my Esha Salaah. I had a dream in which I saw that it was the Day of Qiyaamah and everyone was coming out of their graves. I heard the noise of something following me. I looked back and saw a huge, ugly snake coming after me. I started running away to save my life but the snake began chasing me. I saw an old man who was very handsome and smelling of a nice perfume. I made salaam to him and asked him to help me. He started crying and said that he was too weak to help me against such a big snake. He asked me to go to a certain hill where perhaps I would find some help. The snake had come very close to me.

I ran towards the hill and saw that it contained many windows with curtains of silk. An angel called out, 'Come out of your rooms and see if you can help this man in trouble.' The windows opened and I saw many small children coming out. Amongst them was my daughter who had passed away recently. On seeing me she said, 'By Allah It is my father.' She came to me and I picked her up and hugged her. She pointed towards the snake and it immediately went away. She then made me sit down and sat in my lap. She played with my beard and read the aayat of the Qur-aan which means, *'Has the time not come for the sinful people to change their lives and obey Allah* سُبْحَانَهُ وَتَعَالَى*?'* I started crying and asked my daughter, 'Do all of you know the meaning of the Qur-aan?' She replied, 'Yes! We know it better than you.' I asked, 'My dear child! What was that snake?' She said, 'It is the shape of your sins. The snake is very strong. It is you who has done so many sins. It was about to catch you and throw you into Jahannam.' I asked, 'Who was that old, handsome man?' She said, 'That is your good deeds which has become very weak because you did so little good deeds. That is why it could not help you against the snake.' I asked, 'What are you all doing on this hill?' She replied, 'We are the children of the Muslims who died when we were small. We shall wait here until the Day of Qiyaamah when we will be joined with our parents and we will help them if they are in trouble.'

I then woke up still very scared of that big snake. I regretted over my life of sin and turned to Allah سُبْحَانَهُ وَتَعَالَى begging Him to forgive me. I then left out all sins and began to obey Allah سُبْحَانَهُ وَتَعَالَى.

DEATH

قَالَ رَسُوْلُ اللهِ صَلَّى اللهُ عَلَيْهِ وَسَلَّمَ

اَكْثِرُوْا ذِكْرَ هَاذِمِ اللَّذَّاتِ يَعْنِي اَلْمَوْتَ

Increase in the remembrance of the destroyer of all pleasures (death). (Remember death more often)

[Tirmizi]

Lessons Learnt

1. A person who is enjoying the pleasures of this life forgets that he will have to die.

2. Death will bring an end to the pleasures of life in this world.

3. We should prepare ourselves for the life of the hereafter by thinking of death all the time.

4. The actions of a person will accompany him in the hereafter.

5. We should always do such actions that will help us in the Hereafter.

There was once a man who collected a lot of wealth. He built a beautiful palace for himself and arranged all types of comforts and luxuries in it. When he moved into the palace, he organised a feast for his friends and relatives. When everyone sat down for meals, he sat on a throne and thought to himself that he has a lot of things which will last for years. While he was thinking these thoughts, a beggar came and knocked on the door so loudly that it disturbed all the guests who were eating.

The servants rushed to the door to see who was causing the disturbance. When they saw this person, they asked him what he wanted. He said, "Send your master to me." They said, "Do you think our master is going to come out to see you?" The man said, "He will come. Go and tell him." When they went and told their master about it, he said, "Why didn't you all give him a good hiding and send him away for being so rude?" As he said this, the man started knocking even louder. The servants again rushed to the door. The man said, "Tell your master that I am Izraeel, the angel of death." The servants were shocked and when they told their master, he was stunned and humbly said, "Ask him to take someone else in my place."

The angel, who had entered the palace already, said, "You can do what you want but I cannot go back until I take your soul out of your body." The rich man gathered his wealth and said, "Curses upon you, O wretched wealth! You kept me too busy to remember and worship Allah سُبْحَانَهُوَتَعَالَى." Allah سُبْحَانَهُوَتَعَالَى granted his wealth the power to speak and it said to him, "Why do you curse me? It was because of me that you could go into the courts of kings when the poor were chased away. It was because of me that women came to you and you used to do haraam with them. You spent me on haraam and I was helpless in your hands. Had you spent me on good, I would have helped you." In the middle of this conversation, the angel of death pulled out the soul from his body. This was the bad ending for the one who forgot death.

Story 56

A king once decided to visit his kingdom. A suit of clothes was brought to him but he rejected it. Another was brought but he also rejected it . After rejecting many different suits of clothing, he finally chose one. He wore this smart suit and called for a horse. A fine horse was brought but he rejected it. Another was brought which he also rejected. An entire stable of horses was brought before him and he selected the best horse. The king then sat on the horse and rode off followed by his friends, ministers and soldiers. Shaytaan made him feel very proud and better than everyone else. As he rode on, he saw an old man who was dressed in rags. The old man greeted the king but the king ignored him. The old man caught hold of the horse's bridle. This greatly angered the king who said, "Off with you. How dare you catch hold of my horse's reins?" The man said, "I have some business with you." The king said, "Be patient and wait till I return for then I shall have time to listen to what you have to say." The man said, "I must say it now." He then pulled the horse towards him. The king asked, "Well, what do you want to say?" The man said, "It is a secret, I must whisper it in your ears." The king lowered his head and the man whispered in his ears, "I am the Angel of Death and I have come to take your soul." The king became afraid and said in a shaky voice, "Please give me some time to go home, meet my family and arrange my things." The angel said, "No, you shall have no more time. Never again shall you meet your people or see your things." Saying this, the Angel of Death pulled out the soul from his body and he fell down from the horse like a log of dry wood.

After this, the Angel of Death went to a pious man who was also on a journey. The angel greeted him with Salaam and the man replied with Salaam. The angel said to him, "I want to say something in your ear. I am the Angel of Death." The man said, "Most welcome! Blessed is your visit! I have been waiting for you for a very long time. Of all the people who were away from me, I was most anxious to meet you." The angel said, "Go and quickly finish off whatever work you have to do." The man said, "I would dearly love to meet my Allah سُبْحَانَهُوَتَعَالَى more than anything else in the world." The angel said, "Choose for yourself any way in which you would like to die. I shall remove your soul in that way." The man said, "Let me make wudhu and stand in salaah. When I am in Sajdah, take my life away." The pious man began his Salaah and when he went into Sajdah, his soul was taken out of his body.

Grade One

Tick		قَالَ رَسُوْلُ اللهِ صَلَّى اللهُ عَلَيْهِ وَسَلَّمَ	
	Say *Assalaamu alykum* before you begin speaking.	اَلسَّلَامُ قَبْلَ الْكَلَامِ	1.
	Be truthful.	عَلَيْكُمْ بِالصِّدْقِ	2.
	Take good care of the Qur-aan.	تَعَاهَدُوا الْقُرْآنَ	3.
	Do not spy.	لَا تَجَسَّسُوا	4.
	Feed the hungry.	أَطْعِمُوا الْجَائِعَ	5.

Grade Two

Tick	قَالَ رَسُوْلُ اللهِ صَلَّى اللهُ عَلَيْهِ وَسَلَّمَ	
	Cleanliness is half of Imaan. (faith)	اَلطُّهُوْرُ شَطْرُ الْاِيْمَانِ	6.
	Salaah is a pillar of Deen.	اَلصَّلوةُ عِمَادُ الدِّيْنِ	7.
	The best type of Zikr is "**Laa ilaha illallah**".	اَفْضَلُ الذِّكْرِ لَا اِلٰهَ اِلَّا اللهُ	8.
	The best person is one who benefits other people.	خَيْرُ النَّاسِ اَنْفَعُهُمْ لِلنَّاسِ	9.
	Swearing a Muslim is a major sin.	سِبَابُ الْمُسْلِمِ فُسُوْقٌ	10.

Grade Three

Tick		قَالَ رَسُوْلُ اللهِ صَلَّى اللهُ عَلَيْهِ وَسَلَّمَ
	Jannah is under the feet of the mothers.	اَلْجَنَّةُ تَحْتَ أَقْدَامِ الْأُمَّهَاتِ — 11.
	Allah سُبْحَانَهُ وَتَعَالَى is angry with a person whose father is angry with him.	سَخْطُ الرَّبِّ فِي سَخْطِ الْوَالِدِ — 12.
	Do not hate one another.	لَا تَبَاغَضُوْا — 13.
	Save yourself from backbiting.	إِيَّاكُمْ وَالْغِيْبَةَ — 14.
	Visit the sick.	عُوْدُوا الْمَرِيْضَ — 15.
	Seeking knowledge is the compulsory duty of every Muslim.	طَلَبُ الْعِلْمِ فَرِيْضَةٌ عَلَى كُلِّ مُسْلِمٍ — 16.

Grade Four

Tick		
	قَالَ رَسُوْلُ اللهِ صَلَّى اللهُ عَلَيْهِ وَسَلَّمَ	
	Certainly, actions depend on their intentions.	اِنَّمَا الْاَعْمَالُ بِالنِّيَّاتِ	17.
	Do not choose anybody to be your friend except someone who is a Muslim.	لَا تُصَاحِبْ اِلَّا مُؤْمِنًا	18.
	Guard your tongue.	اَمْلِكْ عَلَيْكَ لِسَانَكَ	19.
	Save yourself from jealousy.	اِيَّاكُمْ وَ الْحَسَدَ	20.
	Avoid anger.	اِجْتَنِبُوا الْغَضَب	21.
	Allah سُبْحَانَهُ وَتَعَالَى does not show mercy to him who does not show mercy to others.	لَا يَرْحَمُ اللهُ مَنْ لَّا يَرْحَمُ النَّاسَ	22.

Grade Five

Tick	قَالَ رَسُوْلُ اللهِ صَلَّى اللهُ عَلَيْهِ وَسَلَّمَ	
	The best amongst you is he who learns the Qur-aan and teaches it.	خَيْرُكُمْ مَنْ تَعَلَّمَ الْقُرْآنَ وَعَلَّمَهُ	23.
	Treat others with the best of manners.	اَحْسِنْ خُلُقَكَ لِلنَّاسِ	24.
	Modesty is part of Imaan.	اَلْحَيَاءُ شُعْبَةٌ مِّنَ الْاِيْمَانِ	25.
	He who does not thank people cannot thank Allah.	مَنْ لَّمْ يَشْكُرِ النَّاسَ لَمْ يَشْكُرِ اللهَ	26.
	Fear Allah سُبْحَانَهُ وَتَعَالَى wherever you are.	اِتَّقِ اللهَ حَيْثُ مَا كُنْتَ	27.
	One who sends one durood upon me, Allah سُبْحَانَهُ وَتَعَالَى will bless him ten times.	مَنْ صَلَّى عَلَيَّ وَاحِدَةً صَلَّى اللهُ عَلَيْهِ عَشْرًا	28.

Grade Six

Tick	قَالَ رَسُوْلُ اللهِ صَلَّى اللهُ عَلَيْهِ وَسَلَّم	
	Dua is the essence (flavour) of Ibaadah.	اَلدُّعَاءُ مُخُّ الْعِبَادَةِ	29.
	Give gifts to each other you will love each other.	تَهَادَوْا تَحَآبُّوْا	30.
	He who cheats us is not one of us.	مَنْ غَشَّنَا فَلَيْسَ مِنَّا	31.
	Nabi ﷺ was not a rude person nor did he behave rudely.	لَمْ يَكُنْ رَسُوْلُ اللهِ صَلَّى اللهُ عَلَيْهِ وَسَلَّمَ فَاحِشًا وَّلَا مُتَفَحِّشًا	32.
	He who humbles himself for the sake of Allah ﷻ, Allah ﷻ will elevate him in rank.	مَنْ تَوَاضَعَ لِلّٰهِ رَفَعَهُ اللهُ	33.
	The best neighbour in the sight of Allah ﷻ is he who is good to his neighbour.	خَيْرُ الْجِيْرَانِ عِنْدَ اللهِ خَيْرُهُمْ لِجَارِهِ	34.

Grade Seven

Tick			
		قَالَ رَسُوْلُ اللهِ صَلَّى اللهُ عَلَيْهِ وَسَلَّمَ	
	Every Ummah (group of people) had a test. The test of my Ummah is wealth.	اِنَّ لِكُلِّ اُمَّةٍ فِتْنَةً وَّفِتْنَةُ اُمَّتِيَ اَلْمَالُ	35.
	Leave out those things which are doubtful for those things that are not doubtful.	دَعْ مَا يُرِيْبُكَ إِلٰى مَا لَا يُرِيْبُكَ	36.
	All intoxicants are haraam (unlawful).	كُلُّ مُسْكِرٍ حَرَامٌ	37.
	No male should be alone with a strange female.	لَا يَخْلُوَنَّ رَجُلٌ بِامْرَأَةٍ	38.
	Cry over your sins.	وَابْكِ عَلٰى خَطِيْئَتِكَ	39.
	Increase in the remembrance of the destroyer of all pleasures (death). (Remember death more often)	اَكْثِرُوْا ذِكْرَ هَاذِمِ اللَّذَّاتِ يَعْنِي اَلْمَوْتَ	40.

Notes:

www.ingramcontent.com/pod-product-compliance
Lightning Source LLC
LaVergne TN
LVHW041325200726
843509LV00009B/611